"Drawing from her adventures for Christ on the mission field and from her intimate time with the Lord, Julie King takes you on a 40-day journey that could transform your whole outlook on life. Julie has a passion for unreached people groups, has a strong desire to go deeper with Jesus, and is sounding the alarm to get the Body of Christ ready for His imminent return. That's exactly what God wants to do in your life, too! I highly recommend this book. Get one, and give one to your pastor, too!"

Tom Doyle
President, Uncharted Ministries
Author of *Dreams and Visions*, *Standing in the Fire*,
Killing Christians, and co-author of *Women Who Risk*

"If you have read any of Julie King's previous books, you will readily notice a consistent theme. The devotional format will draw the reader to an enlightened focus on a passage of Scripture that will invariably stir one's heart for the mission of God to reach the nations and peoples of the world with the gospel of Jesus Christ. This book, *The Fire Within*, introduces the reader to a dimension of the mission task which the author shares from personal encounters with people living in darkness, hopelessness, and a destitute lifestyle. God still uses signs and wonders today. The Holy Spirit is alive and well, still working miracles of healing and deliverance through a word of faith. It challenges us, as believers, to become a channel of God's power and see the fire of His Spirit work to change lives and be His instrument in bringing the kingdoms of this world to become the Kingdom of our Lord."

Dr. Jerry Rankin, President Emeritus
International Mission Board, SB

"We frequently settle for less than God's full plan for our lives. He saved us from darkness, adopted us into His family, and invited us to participate in His wonderful redemptive plan. Unfortunately, we've lost the narrative, allowing the almighty self to emerge as the central actor in God's unfolding drama. We, like princes and princesses in rags counting pennies, obsess over temporal security or transient things while ignoring our divine inheritance. Enter *The Fire Within*. This book recalibrates our attention on eternity, helping us to discover our role in God's global plan. Read this book with an open heart and ready feet, ready to embark on an adventure beyond your wildest dreams."

David Joannes, Founder/CEO
Within Reach Global
Author of *The Mind of a Missionary*

"The Fire Within is more than a devotional—it is an invitation to renewal. In these pages, you will be gently and courageously led to examine the places where complacency, fear, or distraction may have dimmed your passion for Jesus and His mission. This 40-day journey creates space for the Spirit to rekindle holy vision, deepen intimacy with Jesus, and restore the urgency of His call to reach a world in need.

"What I appreciate most about this resource is its balance of personal transformation and outward focus. True revival always begins in the heart, but it never stays there. As you walk through these reflections, prayers, and challenges, you will find yourself not only drawn closer to the heart of Jesus but also commissioned afresh to join Him in His work among the nations.

"For anyone longing to move from spiritual routine to spiritual fire, this book offers a clear and faithful pathway. My prayer is that the Lord will use these 40 days to ignite a deeper love for Him, a renewed surrender to His purposes, and a bold compassion for those who have yet to hear His name."

Kristen Shuler, President
East-West

"As soon as you embrace *The Fire Within*, expect a burning for the Messiah to be rekindled within your heart. It won't take long! There is a newness that will stir in your soul. Forty days of pressing intentionally in with the Word of God will help prepare you for the return of Jesus. Yes, Lord!

"The logs of repentance will burn off old ways of living. The embers of revival will ignite the flames of pursuing Him, and the flames of obedience will bring refreshment to responding to His voice.

"This book will spur you on, as it did for me, to live out what you believe. And without a question, you won't be able to stay quiet. As the psalmist David wrote, *'My heart grew hot within me; as I mused, a fire burned. I spoke with my tongue … (Psalm 39:3, CSB).'*

"Please be prepared. *The Fire Within* will create a personal desire to actively declare who Jesus is in your life. And with passion and zeal, you will be encouraged to invite others to know Him in a refreshing manner. The fire will burn brighter within, and others will be drawn to the light of Christ in your life. All for His glory!"

Dr. Kyle Lance Martin
Founder of Time to Revive

"For the past seven years, I've had the privilege of knowing Julie King as a beloved ministry leader and woman wholly surrendered to Jesus. Julie is fiercely committed to taking the gospel to a world that so desperately needs Jesus. I have watched Julie embrace her calling with a steady, unwavering flame that does not flicker with circumstance. The passion that marks her prayers, her writing, and her pursuit of the lost is authentic and intentional. It is the same fire that breathes through every page of this beautiful devotional.

"I am honored to stand beside her as she equips and raises up women to step boldly into their Great Commission calling. Julie faithfully directs hearts back to Jesus with clarity, humility, and conviction. What you hold in your hands is born from years of prayer, surrender, and praise to the Spirit of God.

"*The Fire Within* is a gift. I encourage you to enter this 40-day journey with openness and expectation. Allow the Lord to use these pages to stretch you, refine you, and call you higher. Steward this message with a heart postured in submission to the Holy Spirit's leading in your life.

"I join my dear friend Julie in praying that *The Fire Within* ignites holy urgency, awakens what may have grown dormant, and mobilizes believers to fully yield to Christ. This message is timely, necessary, and anointed for this critical hour in the calling of the Church to the world. To God be the glory!"

Cindy Brinker Simmons
Businesswoman, Author, and Community Leader

THE FIRE

Within

A 40-Day Revival Journey

JULIE KING

*A Call to Awaken Holy Fire and Live Sent
for the Glory of God*

The Fire Within
A 40-Day Revival Journey

Julie King | East-West
To contact the author: julie.king@eastwest.org

For updated information on events, trips, resources, and ways to get involved, visit our website at www.eastwest.org/arise.

ISBN (Print): 979-8-9950731-0-9
ISBN (e-Book): 979-8-9950731-1-6

Published by
East-West
Plano, TX

Other books by Julie King:
Arise My Darling: Encounters with Jesus to Ignite Passion, Worship, and Wonder
Revivalist Arise: Encounters with Jesus that Position You to Carry the Fires of Revival
Arise and Go: The Harvest Has Come

DEDICATION

To the women who have run ahead of me in years and in faith—

You who have traversed decades with Jesus and still say, "Yes," when He calls.

To my Golden Girls- Bunnie, Charlotte, Cheryl, Joy, Lucy, Patti, Rose Ann, and Sandy—

This book is dedicated to you.

Thank you for continuing to Arise, still packing your bags, still stepping onto foreign soil with fire in your bones and eternity in your hearts.

You are not slowing down; you are running **toward** your finish line with boldness and courage. You refuse to coast when Heaven is at stake. You show us that obedience does not have an expiration date, that surrender only deepens with time, and that the Great Commission burns just as brightly—if not brighter—in a life fully yielded.

You run with us, not behind us. You cover us with wisdom, laughter, tears, and unshakeable faith. Your yes makes room for generations to follow. Your footsteps are filling Heaven, one gospel encounter at a time.

I honor you. I learn from you. I am stronger because you run beside me.

May your final miles be marked by joy, fruitfulness, and the thunderous welcome of Heaven saying, **"Well done."**

With deep gratitude and holy awe—

Thank you for showing us how to finish strong.

ACKNOWLEDGEMENTS

This book was born in prayer long before it was written in ink. Since 2008, I have been praying for revival, contending for it in different seasons of my life. God has planted within me a holy stirring—a summons to arise, to believe again, and to contend for revival in our day. (And I can say confidently that the Lord is answering this cry of so many who, for generations and decades, have been believing for revival.) I begin with gratitude to Jesus, who is ever faithful to speak, patient to wait, and powerful to fulfill every word He releases. He has been so merciful and so gracious to me. **Thank You for the fire that awakens hearts, for the mercy that revives weary souls, and for the gospel that still changes the world. This work belongs to You.**

To my family—thank you for living this calling with me. Mom and Dad, I stand on your shoulders of faith. Mike, thank you for interceding for me and loving me in my imperfections. You show me the grace and love of God so beautifully. You have carried the weight and the wonder of obedience, often behind the scenes, always with grace. Thank you for your prayers, your sacrifices, your flexibility, and your unwavering support as this message was formed in the quiet, morning by morning, and released in faith. My precious girls, I pray that you will take my mantle and go boldly into the world!

To my personal missionary support team, you have covered my life and this ministry; your generosity and prayers have sustained me more than you know. You believed in the call of God on my life and helped to fuel that. This book carries the fruit of your faithfulness.

To my besties who love me faithfully and shoulder this calling with me (even from afar)—you are a gift in my life and I love you.

To our Arise leaders across the nation—thank you for saying, "Yes," to the vision of seeing women mobilized, nations reached, and the gospel proclaimed in some of the darkest and most unreached places on Earth. You are co-laborers in this work. Every testimony, every life transformed, every seed planted across the nations is because you chose to invest, pray, and believe that obedience still matters. Melissa, thank you for holding us together.

East-West leaders—Kurt, Kristen, Paul, Chip, Don, Michael, and Scott—you each have made a profound deposit in my life, and I honor you for modeling humble and excellent leadership.

To the women on the frontlines—those who have gone, those who are preparing to go, and those who are discovering their Great Commission calling—this book was written with you in mind. Your courage fuels my faith. Your yes echoes louder than you realize.

To the team who helped bring this book from revelation to reality— Mary Ethel Eckard and the marketing team at East-West—thank you for stewarding this message with excellence and care. Your diligence has helped carry this word to the hands and hearts it is meant to reach.

And to you, the reader—thank you for your hunger. If you are holding this book, it is because God is stirring something within you. My prayer is that these pages would awaken holy expectancy, strengthen your resolve, and remind you that revival is not a distant memory or future hope—it is a present invitation. **May you arise, be filled with fresh fire, and carry the gospel boldly into the world God has placed before you.**

No calling is fulfilled alone. This book stands as a testimony to what God can do through yielded hearts, faithful partnership, and obedient faith. May He revive us again—for His glory, and for the sake of the nations.

CONTENTS

FOREWORD

I have had the privilege of walking alongside Julie King across our nation and around the world. I have witnessed firsthand that the same holy fire that marks her life saturates every page of this book. Julie does not write about revival from a distance—she lives it.

I have watched her run toward the lost with feet that seem to burn with urgency, compassion, and unwavering surrender to Jesus. Her heart for the nations is not theoretical; it is costly, courageous, and deeply rooted in love for the Bride of Christ and for those who have yet to hear the gospel. Whether in remote villages or crowded cities, she remains attentive to the prompting of the Holy Spirit, carrying that intimacy into her writing with clarity and conviction.

In "The Fire Within," Julie invites you into a 40-day journey that is both tender and prophetic, intimate and catalytic. From the opening call to "wash in the Pool of Siloam" (John 9) to the summons toward repentance, consecration, and global commission, this devotional is not meant for passive reading. It is an invitation to awakening.

As Julie writes in the Introduction, there is a call to wash our eyes so that we may truly see and live as those who are sent for the glory of God. That invitation sets the tone for the pages that follow. These devotionals press beyond inspiration and into transformation. They ask difficult questions. They confront comfort. They expose apathy. And they remind us that revival begins not in crowds but in surrendered hearts.

Julie writes as one who has counted the cost. She writes as one who has stood at the altar of fire and allowed the Lord to refine and recommission her. There is no theoretical theology here—only lived conviction. The urgency woven through these pages is not alarmism; it is eternal perspective. It reflects a deep awareness that our time is short, our calling is sacred, and the nations still wait to hear the name of Jesus.

This book calls the Church higher. It summons us back to wholehearted worship, deeper consecration, and steadfast faithfulness. It reminds us that grace is not passive; it transforms. Salvation is not merely security; it is commission. And revival is not emotional excess; it is alignment with the heart of God.

As you begin this 40-day journey, my prayer is simple: that the Lord would ignite within you the same holy hunger that has shaped Julie's life. May spiritual sight be restored. May love for Christ deepen. May your life be marked by courage, surrender, and unwavering devotion to His purposes.

The Church needs this message for such a time as this.

Dr. Alexandria Watkins, DNP-APRN, FNP-C
LiveWell Med Solutions, LLC
Carrollton, Texas

INTRODUCTION

*"As he went along, he saw a man blind from birth. His disciples asked him,
'Rabbi, who sinned, this man or his parents, that he was born blind?'*

*"'Neither this man nor his parents sinned,' said Jesus, 'but this happened
so that the works of God might be displayed in him. **As long as it is day,
we must do the works of him who sent me. Night is coming, when
no one can work.** While I am in the world, I am the light of the world.'*

*"After saying this, he spit on the ground, made some mud
with the saliva, and put it on the man's eyes. 'Go,' he told
him, 'wash in the Pool of Siloam' (this word means 'Sent').
So the man went and washed, and came home seeing."*
—John 9:1–7, emphasis added

A significant journey is about to begin and, in my spirit, I sense this invitation from the Lord to "wash in the Pool of Siloam" before we cross over into this revival pursuit over the next 40 days.

Here sits a man born blind. Every day, his world was dark and colorless. He never saw what everyone else saw. I can imagine he learned to see with his other senses, but his world would only be as large as those who would explore it with him. I doubt he ever thought, "One day, my life will bring glory to God." I doubt he wondered what day he would be healed and would run free. What did running free even mean? That day seemed like just another day, no different than the rest—limited and small.

But here came Jesus, walking up to the man, not the other way around. And He did something so unique for this man. Spitting in the dust, the very substance from which man was created, Jesus did a new thing in this man's life. There was no formulaic method to Jesus' healing; He simply responded to the leadership of the Father to the needs of those who stood before Him.

And now the man had to respond in faith. He had to do something with the command of Christ to go and wash. Grabbing the hand of a friend, he had to find his way to the pool of Siloam in order to wash the mud from his eyes. Why? This moment would need the partnership of the man's faith and obedience. Hope said, "Something could change," and faith said, "Someone take me to the pool." Obedience put one foot in front of the other.

When Jesus shows up while we can't see, hope is restored, faith for impossibility is deposited in us, and faithful obedience becomes the fruit— and the whole town knows!

The Pool of Siloam's water came through Hezekiah's tunnel, which William Barclay noted was a remarkable engineering feat for the equipment available in Old Testament times.

> "It was called Siloam, which, it was said, meant sent, because the water in it had been sent through the conduit into the city." –William Barclay

So, what is Jesus inviting us to do as we enter these next 40 days of our revival journey?

I believe many of us have lost our sight. We've lost sight of Jesus, and as we live in such a myopic culture, I believe the Church has lost sight that there is an entire world existing outside of America that sits in darkness and oppression. We've lost sight of the fact that eternity is our glorious

JULIE KING

destination. Has our vision been skewed by the taunts of the enemy to long for wealth and comfort more than anything of eternal value? Do we simply see only farther than our two feet when there's a 360-degree perspective God is asking us to look at? I ask these rhetorical questions from a place of my own struggle and observation, not judgment. I don't hold any stones in my hand.

There is a pull at our hearts to seek comfort and wealth and stability that trumps a call to faith and obedience. Our entire culture is tied to this reality. Yet as a follower of Jesus, we are to live counter-culturally. How do we maintain both perspectives? I don't believe we can. Right in the middle of this passage in John, Jesus obstructs our view: *"As long as it is day, we must do the works of him who sent me. Night is coming, when no one can work (John 9:4)."*

- "Jesus, I can't see You because I'm buried in building a life I always dreamed I deserved."
- "Jesus, I can't make my way to the pool to wash because I don't know if You're really going to follow through; hope deferred has sabotaged my heart of faith."
- "Jesus, I am comfortable with my life of lack and blindness because then I won't be responsible for more than You might ask me to do. I'm afraid of what You could really be calling me to."

Beloved, we have got to make our way to the metaphorical Pool of Siloam and wash the barrier off our eyes so we can truly see. We must know the hour in which we are living and the eternal assignment God has placed in our hands. There's no time for the endless pondering of "I don't know what my calling is." It's time for you to see and to know. Jesus wants to reveal your end-time assignments while it is still day. We are His sent ones—sent to a world to proclaim the hope of Jesus. The waters were sent to the city, this man was sent to go from his healing to testify to the power of Jesus, and I can imagine the whole city caught wind of this.

That is what these next 40 days will be about—getting right down to what could be holding us back from a fiery, passionate pursuit of Jesus and the world He died for. We will invite Jesus to do His intimate work to give us new vision and a fire in our bones we can't contain. We will ask Him to commission us afresh over these 40 days.

Jesus is standing at the threshold of this journey, and He's inviting you to head down to the pool to wash your eyes. We want to see what He has in store for you. Let's wash off hesitancy, doubt, hopelessness, resistance to His calling, and apathy for the lost. Our Bridegroom is coming soon, and we've got a field to harvest all over the world!

May the Lord bless you and keep you and make His face shine upon you! I pray that He will wash our eyes so we can truly see these next 40 days all that God has prepared for those who love Him.

JULIE KING

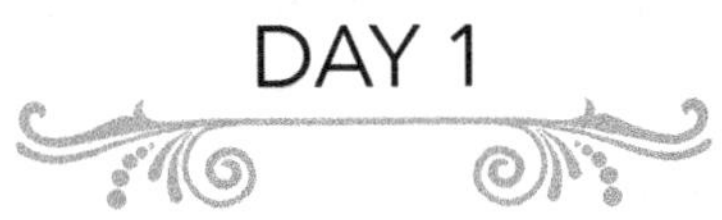

SURVEYING OUR LAND

"Land that drinks in the rain often falling on it and that produces a crop useful to those for whom it is farmed receives the blessing of God."
—Hebrews 6:7

It is my heart to write to you from the places that the Spirit of God is taking me as I pursue Him, as well as what I sense He is speaking in this season. As I look upon the landscape of my life, I want to dream with the Lord for what is next in His assignment for me and for us as we passionately follow Jesus. I want to live my life with vision and faith for the impossible. I want to see revival come in and through my life! I want to see our Church community be a powerful force for the Kingdom of God. We've got one life and one moment to live it all for Him.

Lord, I invite you to increase our intimacy over this next year. I invite you to take us into deeper places of surrender so that Your plans and purposes may be fulfilled in our lives.

As I read the verse in Hebrews, I asked the Lord the following questions:

What is the condition of my land—all that God has assigned to me?

Does the land of my life bear fruit to the extent God has intended?

Do I position my heart to be softened to receive the Spirit's
words to me?
Are there any places that are hard or fallow ground?

Let us prepare for rain! He longs to open Heaven and pour out rain
to make us fruitful, bearing witness to the world of the faithfulness and
power of God! It's time to dream again and ask the Lord, "Why on Earth
did you make me and put me in this moment of history? Is my life bearing
the fruitfulness you have created me for?"

*"Even when their paths wind through the dark valley of tears, they
dig deep to find a pleasant pool where others find only pain. He gives
to them a brook of blessing filled from the rain of an outpouring."*
—Psalm 84:6, TPT

*"'I will make rivers flow on barren heights, and springs
within the valleys. I will turn the desert into pools of
water, and the parched ground into springs.'"*
—Isaiah 41:18

For those of us who see land in our lives that has been parched and
barren, it can be drenched with the rain of Heaven so it produces life once
again. If you are in a season of distraction, disappointment, or pain, please
don't check out. It's time to dream with God for all that He will fulfill in
the plans He has written over your life. Revival is about positioning our
hearts before Him in surrender as we consecrate ourselves afresh to Him.

For those of you who have been reading these devotionals since 2020,
you are familiar with the message of exhortation to the Church through
my writings:

- We live with an urgency to take the gospel to the nations.
- We live with an ever-present reality that Jesus is coming soon for
  His Bride.

     JULIE KING

- We live with the knowledge of the billions who have yet to hear the name of Jesus.

None of those messages are shifting. In fact, we are going to seek deeper understanding and greater application. **This is our year to ask that the rain of Heaven intersects the fire of the Spirit to produce revival in us and through us. That will be our pursuit this year.** These 40 devotionals call us to pursue revival personally and globally. God is doing this all over the world, and I want us to be front and center, knee-deep in His work.

So pray with me the very prayer I have scribed in my own journal:

> Jesus, place Your hand on the land of my life and pour out Your Spirit. Break up any fallow ground. Water what You have planted so that it bears much fruit. Let a harvest come forth. Produce a crop in my life for Your glory and for all of eternity. Lord, uproot the weeds. Pull out the people on my land who have no business being there. Will You station angels on my land to minister and to war against the enemy? Will You remove any false "land owners" who are squatting on my land and are not permitted to be there? Will You receive the crops of my life as a sacrifice of worship and praise, no matter what it costs me? This land of my life belongs to You. Pour out revival, Lord!

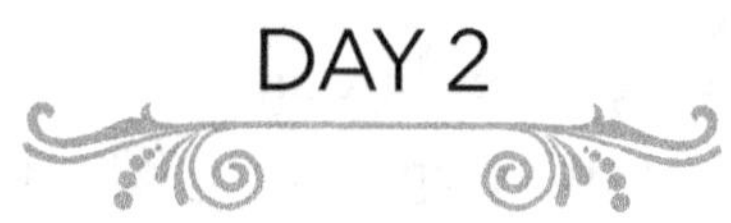

THE BIRTHPLACE OF REVIVAL

*"'… if my people, who are called by my name, will humble themselves
and pray and seek my face and turn from their wicked ways, then I will
hear from heaven, and I will forgive their sin and will heal their land.'"*
—2 Chronicles 7:14

"'Yet he has not left himself without testimony:
He has shown kindness by giving you rain from heaven and crops
in their seasons; he provides you with plenty of
food and fills your hearts with joy.'"
—Acts 14:17

"'Bring the whole tithe into the storehouse, that there may be food
in my house. Test me in this,' says the Lord Almighty, 'and see if
I will not throw open the floodgates of heaven and pour out so
much blessing that there will not be room enough to store it.'"
—Malachi 3:10

I believe with all of my heart that this is going to be a year of great intentionality of God's people, as He awakens us and as we press in together to align our hearts with the heart of God. I see so many of us on our knees before the Lord, hands outstretched and hearts positioned in deep surrender. We are no longer satisfied with old messages and yesterday's *rhema* word. We don't want yesterday's testimony of God's miracles. We want a fresh word from the Spirit and a new move of God we have never seen. New pages of history and testimony are yet to be written. All the while, we are being clothed in glorious garments of humility and holiness.

My writings in this devotional are on pursuing the heart of revival and awakening so that our lives overflow with the fire and love of Jesus.

Most revivals throughout history have documented that prayer was the starting point of a massive move of God. But I would like to propose that it was even more intimate and sacred than that. It took someone being moved by the Spirit, getting hungry, desperate, and surrendered. It was in a quiet whisper to the Lord, a tender place of worship, or a mustard seed of faith to give God their yes—just a turning to align their heart with the heart of God that caused something to break forth. And then God began to download blueprints.

There is no algorithm to revival that can be followed. God is intimately and uniquely moving in the Earth. But He's looking for the ones who will get real, honest, humble, and repentant so that He can do something in and through them that Heaven is longing to release. Pages of history have yet to be written through these ones!

He invites us to bring our tithe—something that costs us, something we must sacrifice to the Lord. He longs to pour out on His people an abundance of His glorious riches in Christ Jesus from this place of sacrifice and surrendered worship. **I pray that the floodgates of blessing on our land will be for the advancement of the gospel across the Earth.** I pray that we would see the glory of God cover the Earth from the remnant of God's people living and breathing in this place of surrendered worship.

> "Revival is simply New Testament Christianity, the saints
> going back to normal." –Vance Havner

We can study revival from past history and glean our treasures so that our faith rises. But what if God wants to do something in our day we have never seen? What if He wants to write a new story that has never been told? What if this breed of fiery lovers of Jesus prays for a move of the Spirit that goes further and faster than our eyes have ever seen? We can pray, "Do it again," or we can ask Him to do something history has never seen so that hearts awaken throughout the Earth. Either of these prayers has to come from a place of desperation and worship of the One who longs to pour out fresh rain on desperate ground. His storehouse is bursting at the seams with abundance!

I write these words with a longing to see the nations turn to Jesus. I write these words with an increased aching to meet Jesus in the clouds. The urgency for the hour pulsates through my veins and, I pray, in yours as well.

Lord, in humility, repentance, and desperation, I come.
Do in me something of such deep surrender and consecration that my life will be marked for all of eternity.
Clothe me in garments of humility and holiness.
Pour out revival across the Earth, beginning in me.
God, give us the nations.

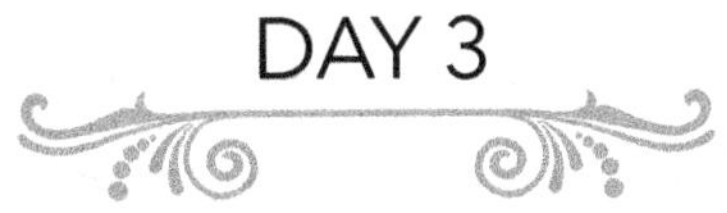

GET READY FOR ADVANCEMENT

"He makes winds his messengers, flames of fire his servants."
—Psalm 104:4

"'But you will receive power when the Holy Spirit comes on you; and you will be my witnesses in Jerusalem, and in all Judea and Samaria, and to the ends of the earth.'"
—Acts 1:8

"Therefore, since we are receiving a kingdom that cannot be shaken, let us be thankful, and so worship God acceptably with reverence and awe, for our 'God is a consuming fire.'"
—Hebrews 12:28–29

Prior to the inauguration of our nation's 47th president, I heard Christian leaders proclaiming that America is entering her "golden age," where wealth will abound and prosperity will flourish. During his inauguration speech, Donald Trump declared, "The golden age of America begins right now." Meanwhile, I want to shout from the rooftops, "Church, advance!" This is not the time to store up treasures for ourselves or build bigger barns (Luke 12:16–21). It's not the time to relax and lose sight of our mission. It's time to move forward with the gospel—urgently, boldly, and with focus.

Many Christian leaders wonder if the Church in America has lost her global vision. In my observation, I fear we've grown comfortable, content to sit in a holy huddle doing decades of Bible studies all while neglecting the nations. We often leave the work of global missions to others—nations like South Korea or Mongolia—while excusing ourselves with local efforts that barely scratch the surface of true evangelism.

My concern deepens when Christian leaders preach a message of prosperity and peace, implying that we can afford to be at ease. In 2024, it seemed like eschatological events, like those outlined in Ezekiel 38 and 39 (a future prophetic war of five nations coming against Israel), were unfolding before our eyes. Scripture was coming alive, and many of us sensed the seriousness of the times. But now, with talk of "peace and safety" (1 Thessalonians 5:3) in this "golden era," how are we to respond?

We must resist the urge to be lulled into complacency. The Church must awaken to her mission. We live in turbulent times. The signs point us toward urgency, not comfort. As followers of Christ, we are called to carry the gospel to the ends of the Earth, not retreat into personal ease or self-preservation.

If He has placed eternity in our hearts, then how are we to spend our time? With an increase of access to the gospel on a global scale, there are still areas and people groups who have never heard the name of Jesus.

Will you go and tell them about Jesus?

Last year, I walked into a village in South Asia, which was home to an unengaged unreached people group. The tribe needed a triple language translation from English to Urdu to their tribal dialect as we shared the gospel. I watched as little 6-year-old girls were married to men in their 40s. Pedophilia and abuse ran rampant in this village. They were considered slaves to the landowners and the scum of the Earth in that country. They were poor, thirsty, blind, and spiritually dead. As I surveyed the scene, it was more than my heart could contain. I looked into the eyes of deeply abused women and saw that they had given up the very will to live. One man (who we thought brought his daughter into the medical clinic) said this little girl had stopped speaking and eating. She was so frail. Come to find out, she was his wife, not his little 6-year-old daughter. My heart was wrecked. But Jesus came that day, and many gave their lives to Him! There is hope for that village now. But there are 30 similar tribes in that area just like this one, waiting to hear about Jesus. Would you go to them if Jesus asked you to?

My husband, Mike, has been turned inside out in reading the life of Dietrich Bonhoeffer. Quotes such as the following have deeply moved him:

> "One act of obedience is better than one hundred sermons."
> "Only he who believes is obedient, and only he who is obedient believes."
> "We must be ready to allow ourselves to be interrupted by God."
> "When Christ calls a man, he bids him come and die."

Mike has said to me in his honest processing, "Faith has to cost us something." He confessed one night over dinner that he has lived his life in the convenience of what he has wanted or not wanted to do as it pertained to the gospel. He admits to having it wrong all of his life. He realized that no one has ever made an impact for the gospel by just doing endless Bible studies. No one in Scripture became worthy of the Bible based on all of their head knowledge but rather their faith lived out in action to advance the gospel! Now, God gets to answer the "Now what?" as Mike walks this out with Jesus.

Church, I beseech you with all of my heart to get to the deepest place of surrender so that, just like in the Scriptures I opened this devotional with, the Spirit may be poured out as God calls you to advance. I want to be a servant with the fire of the Holy Spirit residing greatly in my life, consumed by His presence and living out His purposes. Do you? Could this be a time that we partner with the Spirit to release the Kingdom of God in even greater measure so that the glory of God advances even further to cover more of the Earth?

Make this servant a flame of fire in this moment of history, in the name of Jesus!

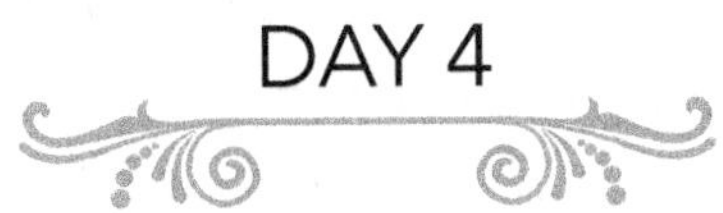

EARNEST AWAITERS

"And you, my child, will be called a prophet of the Most High; for you will go on before the Lord to prepare the way for him, to give his people the knowledge of salvation through the forgiveness of their sins, because of the tender mercy of our God, by which the rising sun will come to us from heaven to shine on those living in darkness and in the shadow of death, to guide our feet into the path of peace."
—Luke 1:76–79

"The people were waiting expectantly and were all wondering in their hearts if John might possibly be the Messiah. John answered them all, 'I baptize you with water. But one who is more powerful than I will come, the straps of whose sandals I am not worthy to untie. He will baptize you with the Holy Spirit and fire. His winnowing fork is in his hand to clear his threshing floor and to gather the wheat into his barn, but he will burn up the chaff with unquenchable fire.'"
—Luke 3:15–17

I have a dear friend, Joy, who travels with me all over the world. She loves to preach the gospel. But what makes her heart surge with life is keeping her eyes upward, awaiting the return of her soon-coming

King. She is 82 and has taught the Bible her whole life. For the past six years, we have run to the nations together.

There have been moments in my life when I think, "Other generations thought Jesus was coming soon, and they passed away." I honestly get weary of holding fast with tenacity and focus. And Joy will remind me over and over not to lose hope. She texted me to say, "I love the term that is used a couple of times in Scripture: 'earnestly awaiting.' We are earnest awaiters!"

Can you imagine 400 years of God not speaking, and the one person God puts on the scene to prepare the way for Jesus is a radical, extremely simple guy who lived on honey and grasshoppers? But he knew how to draw a crowd, and he walked unwaveringly in God's call on his life. His role was to prepare people for the coming Savior.

John the Baptist was an "earnest awaiter" who didn't navel gaze while he stormed the fields for grasshoppers. He had an incredibly important role in getting people ready to encounter Jesus.

Is your role any different in this present age? I would argue, most emphatically, **no**.

John the Baptist knew his God-given mission: to prepare the way for the Lord. John replied in the words of Isaiah the prophet, *"'I am the voice of one calling in the wilderness, "Make straight the way for the Lord (John 1:23).""'*

He lived his entire life readying people for the coming Messiah, keenly aware of his own need for Jesus. John's life teaches us what it truly means to be an "earnest awaiter":

- Focused on God's purposes
- Actively preparing others
- Living with humility and urgency
- Remaining faithful through challenges

John preached repentance. He earnestly called people to turn from sin and prepare their hearts for the arrival of their Savior—a profound revival message! This wasn't a passive waiting but an active preparation in and through John. His life and call to revival are the same for us today in this hour.

He recognized and proclaimed Jesus! *The next day John saw Jesus coming toward him and said, 'Look, the Lamb of God, who takes away the sin of the world (John 1:29)!'*

It is from John's own personal longing and encounter with Jesus that he pointed others to Christ. He helped to shift the gaze of people away from himself and onto Jesus. His life was established in beautiful humility.

> *"He must become greater; I must become less."*
> *–John 3:30*

John lived with urgency and expectation. His sheer separation from the things of the world gave him an intense focus on the things of Christ. As our distractions multiply and the world increases in evil, this is going to have to be an intentional pursuit for God's people.

He suffered for his commitment through both imprisonment and martyrdom. May the words of Philippians 1:21 be the words of our heart: *"For to me, to live is Christ and to die is gain."*

Like John, we too are called to wait expectantly for Christ's return, living in readiness and pointing others to Him. This is our time to prepare the way of the Lord, Church!

> "Her Bridegroom is her life, the joy of her heart. Supremely happy in His love, she is enthralled by her heavenly Bridegroom, spending herself for Him, eagerly awaiting His coming and carrying in her heart this one name: Jesus." –Basilea Schlink, "My All for Him"[1]

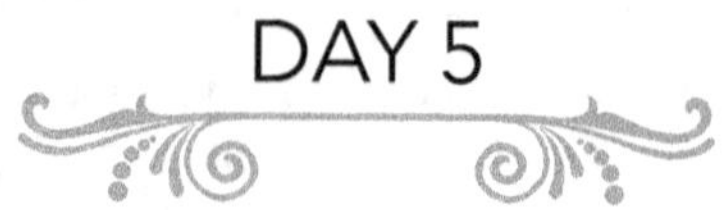

WEDDING CLOTHES

"'Then he said to his servants, "The wedding banquet is ready,
but those I invited did not deserve to come. So go to the street
corners and invite to the banquet anyone you find."
So the servants went out into the streets and
gathered all the people they could find,
bad as well as the good, and the wedding hall was filled with guests.

"'But when the king came in to see the guests, he noticed a man there
*who was not **wearing wedding clothes**. He asked, "How did you get*
in here without wedding clothes, friend?" The man was speechless.'"
—Matthew 22:8–12, emphasis added

When I read this passage, the symbolism of wedding clothes overtakes my thoughts. In this parable, Jesus illustrated the Kingdom of Heaven and the wedding banquet that we will one day experience with Jesus. The king invited many to come and dine at the wedding feast for his son. Those he initially invited refused to come, so he opened the invitation to everyone! However, one guest was found without proper wedding attire.

Am I dressed and ready in my wedding clothes? Am I helping others to be dressed and ready for the coming wedding banquet?

In ancient Jewish weddings, it was customary for the host to provide wedding garments to guests, symbolizing honor and readiness to participate in the celebration. Not wearing the provided attire demonstrated disregard for the host and the occasion. What are these exact garments as symbolized in this passage?

> "'Let us rejoice and be glad and give him glory! For the wedding
> of the Lamb has come, and his bride has made herself ready.
> Fine linen, bright and clean, was given her to wear.' (Fine
> linen stands for the righteous acts of God's holy people.)"
> —Revelation 19:7–8

> "You were taught, with regard to your former way of life, to put
> off your old self, which is being corrupted by its deceitful desires; to
> be made new in the attitude of your minds; and to put on the new
> self, created to be like God in true righteousness and holiness."
> —Ephesians 4:22–24

> "I delight greatly in the Lord; my soul rejoices in my God. For
> he has clothed me with garments of salvation and arrayed me
> in a robe of his righteousness, as a bridegroom adorns his head
> like a priest, and as a bride adorns herself with her jewels."
> —Isaiah 61:10

Followers of Jesus, who have put their trust in Christ and have believed in their hearts and confessed with their mouths that He is Lord, are dressed accordingly. It is upon our salvation that God clothes us in righteousness, holiness, purity, and perfection. We choose, by repentance and receiving salvation, new clean garments that are our wedding clothes.

The man who was spotted at the wedding feast did not have the righteousness of Christ as his garment. He refused to wear the clothes, signifying a rejection of God's provision and a lack of true repentance. Showing up is not enough; we have to receive righteousness on God's terms. It makes me think that he somehow walked through the doors into the wedding feast, looking and sounding the part and blending in easily with all the others who were actually clothed in proper attire. But the king knew; he could see what others could not. What a sobering thought.

> "He came into the banquet when he was bidden, but he came only in appearance, he came not in heart. The banquet was intended for the honour of the son, but this man meant not so; he was willing to eat the good things, but he intended no respect to the prince." –Charles Spurgeon

> *"'Many will say to me on that day, "Lord, Lord, did we not prophesy in your name and in your name drive out demons and in your name perform many miracles?" Then I will tell them plainly, "I never knew you. Away from me, you evildoers!"'"*
> *–Matthew 7:22–23*

Here is what we can glean from this passage with urgency and vision:

The invitation is open to all: Go everywhere you can and invite everyone you can find to get their wedding clothes on so they can attend the wedding of the Lamb one day soon. It's not your job to determine how they respond, but it is your responsibility to tell them about salvation in Jesus.

Readiness requires proper attire: Being part of God's Kingdom requires being clothed with the righteousness of Christ (Romans 13:14). Have you put on the garments of salvation? Showing up in God's presence is not enough; we must come to Him on His terms.

Grace partners with accountability: While salvation is a gift, God expects us to live in a manner worthy of our calling. Are we being transformed into the likeness of Christ, reflecting His power in and through our surrendered lives? Salvation is not just a ticket to Heaven; it's a life proclaiming and demonstrating the risen Christ!

Lord Jesus, get us ready in our spirits, with urgency, for our soon-coming King! I pray you would transform Your people to live in a constant state of preparation for God's Kingdom and not the things of this world. Make us bold in this hour to warn those who are not yet dressed in wedding attire. Burden us deeply, by Your Spirit, with this reality, and consume us with the power and courage of Your Spirit to head to the highways and byways to invite everyone to come to Jesus! A wedding banquet is just around the corner!

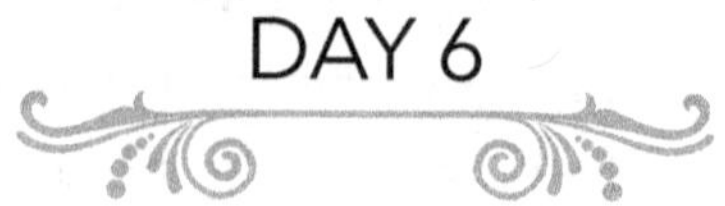

REVIVAL OF WORSHIP

"Sing the praises of the Lord, enthroned in Zion;
proclaim among the nations what he has done."
—Psalm 9:11

"And they cried out in a loud voice: 'Salvation belongs to our God,
who sits on the throne, and to the Lamb.' All the angels were standing
around the throne and around the elders and the four living creatures.
They fell down on their faces before the throne and worshiped God,
saying: 'Amen! Praise and glory and wisdom and thanks and honor
and power and strength be to our God for ever and ever. Amen!'"
—Revelation 7:10–12

I had a profound thought as I was listening to the worship song "Forever YHWH/Worthy Of It All" by Bethel Music and Tiffany Hudson. It left me stunned. **One day, I will be gone, and He will still be worthy of worship.**

Past generations can no longer worship Him here on the Earth, while those unborn cannot yet worship Him. We have but one life to worship Jesus, and when our breath is no longer, our words and life of worship will cease on this side of Heaven. But this is why we were put on the Earth!

So I ask myself this question: Is my whole life given in worship to my King Jesus?

Many of the writings I have scribed over the last five years have to do with the worthiness of Jesus that demands my whole heart's affection and adoration. I have pondered, alongside you, what it looks like to radically pursue and follow Christ. A life laid down is the greatest life of all. But it costs us everything. And I know in seasons, the cost feels too great. I can feel weary of storming the gates of Hell and having the enemy try to punish such a calculated life for the gospel. But would I—would we—want to live for anything else? I have learned to thank God that there's a target on my back because I would rather live for Christ than live and die for nothing.

> "Everything created in the world should be seen in the context of existing for God's glory. Every activity and endeavor should be to glorify Him not only in our lives and community but among all peoples, even to the ends of the earth." –Jerry Rankin, "Spiritual Warfare and Missions"[2]

If we want to see revival come to America and the nations, our worship must begin to shift. We weren't made to worship man or things or money or self; we were made to worship Christ alone! When we bow before the throne of God one day, everything in Heaven and on Earth will bend its knee. If Earth is a dress rehearsal for Heaven, what are we waiting for? We can't pray or hope for revival if our worship of Jesus is out of alignment. For far too long, we have enjoyed the worship of God and everything else our souls and bodies desire. We get to call the shots because we have free will, and we rest in the reality of grace and the promise of eternity, and yet America drifts further and further away from God. It's time to return to a life of worship—the great exchange of my death for His abundant life (Galatians 2:20).

If we knew we had just two more days, and then our testimony of following Christ, no matter what it cost us, came to an end, how would we live? Our story would end with a final punctuation mark. Our legacy would be done. Would anyone say of me, "She lived her whole life in worship to Jesus; every breath mattered in her precious life"?

Revival will come through even just one person when you and I choose to live a life of worship for the One who gave everything so we could have life.

Today, Lord, I ask You to bring forth revival through a passionate cry to make me a worshipper. All of my life, laid down in worship to You. I give You this life as a living sacrifice, holy and pleasing to You. This is my act of worship today. Shift the places in my heart that worship anything other than You so that my life comes into full alignment with Your heart, Your will, and Your purposes. In the glorious name of Jesus!

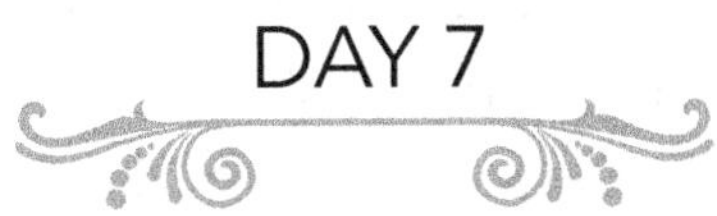

A TIME FOR REPENTANCE

"'Now, fellow Israelites, I know that you acted in ignorance, as did your leaders. But this is how God fulfilled what he had foretold through all the prophets, saying that his Messiah would suffer. **Repent, then, and turn to God, so that your sins may be wiped out, that times of refreshing may come from the Lord,** *and that he may send the Messiah, who has been appointed for you—even Jesus. Heaven must receive him until the time comes for God to restore everything, as he promised long ago through his holy prophets.'"*
–Acts 3:17–21, emphasis added

As we forge a pursuit of revival, one of the gold strands that is woven throughout revival is the glorious gift of repentance. It's a recognition of our responsibility, sin, rebellion, and even disengagement from the Lord. Repentance is such a profound gift to God's people so that we can return again and again and receive the refreshing and healing we need from Jesus.

In this particular passage in Acts, Peter pleaded with those who already thought they belonged to God. These Jews who gathered believed they were righteous because they obeyed the law and made sacrifices for their sin—religion, steeped in the law but devoid of the real power to save them. In a bold and clear call, he pleaded with them that although they acted in ignorance, they were still guilty of their sin. But the good news of the matter is that the sovereign will of God to send His Son fulfills the prophetic expectations of the Old Testament. Nothing happened outside of God's plan for a perfect sacrifice to die in their place. Jesus made the way for their righteousness before God, and they now had an opportunity to respond in repentance.

The words the Lord has spoken into my spirit over and over are "deeper consecration." I have set my heart on asking the Lord to daily circumcise my heart and cut away everything that doesn't belong—every attention, affection, and attitude of my heart not directed wholly at Jesus. Oftentimes, I will take communion daily to worship and apply the cross and resurrection to every part of my life. I don't want any rock unturned in my heart. As the world grows darker and much of the Church blends into culture, I so long that my first love remains attached to the One who gave His life for me. I long to burn with a passionate fire for Jesus with my lamp filled with fresh-pressed oil.

> *"'You have persevered and have endured hardships for my name, and have not grown weary. Yet I hold this against you: You have forsaken the love you had at first. Consider how far you have fallen! Repent and do the things you did at first. If you do not repent, I will come to you and remove your lampstand from its place.'"*
> *—Revelation 2:3–5*

Peter's urgent plea in Acts 3 to the religious of his day applies to us: repent and do a 180 in your thoughts and actions. It's time to turn (back) to God for salvation so that refreshing can come because the great and glorious day of Jesus is coming. The return of Jesus was imminent for Peter in his perspective, as it should be for us.

According to Strong's Exhaustive Concordance, "refreshing" indicates "a recovery of breath," figuratively known as revival. When we understand the supernatural gift and blessings of repentance, I think we would be more apt to run there more quickly. Breathe, oh breath of God, into Your Bride, that we would truly live!

Our sins have been forgiven because of the cross. He paid it all that we would stand in the perfect righteousness of Christ. But the apathy and secularism of our Christianity in America needs repentance. **We need a returning so that refreshing can come. He longs to restore and revive that which has died because of the effects of sin.**

I want to close with this beautiful prayer of repentance in case there is something the Holy Spirit is highlighting to you that needs to be put under the blood of Jesus. It is taken from Peter Louis's book, "Back to the Gospel."[3]

"Father, I know you forgive me because you have committed to doing so, but I want to come to you and ask for your forgiveness for this thing I have done. I hate this behavior that somehow keeps plaguing me. As a new creation in Christ, your son (or daughter), I despise this sinful behavior and want nothing to do with it. This is destructive and harmful behavior that I was never created for. Because of the cleansing and renewing blood of Jesus, I understand that this sin that manifested in me is not who I really am. Thank you that I have your permission to consider myself dead to it and alive to you! I am no longer a debtor to my flesh (Rom. 8:12) or have any obligation to honor the desires my flesh presents to me. Father, I simply put off this sinful behavior. I declare that I am not a victim of a sinful nature and am no longer prone to wander from you. Holy Spirit, renew my mind and help me to see myself as the Father sees me, even in the wake of my actions. By faith, I choose to put on my new self, which was created after the very likeness of God in true righteousness and holiness (Eph. 4:22-24). In humility, I identify with and receive the godly nature that you have freely given to me by the Holy Spirit.

"I am completely dead to the law. Thank you that your affection and blessings don't come to me because I am perfect, but because I have hidden my life in your Son. Thank you, Jesus, for being my advocate to the Father in this moment. Thank you that you do not distance yourself from me or withhold your love because I screw up. According to your Word, you are drawing close to me to help me overcome this sin. Thank you for your patience and willingness to cleanse me completely from unrighteousness, Jesus. I believe that with you, I died to every last one of my sinful desires and that in every way, by the Spirit of God, I am alive to the Father!"

Let us return to the Lord in repentance so that refreshing and revival can come to the Bride of Christ, in the name of Jesus! We are desperate for you, Jesus. Maranatha!

AN ALTAR OF FIRE

"Then the disciple whom Jesus loved said to Peter, 'It is the Lord!' As soon as Simon Peter heard him say, 'It is the Lord,' he wrapped his outer garment around him (for he had taken it off) and jumped into the water. The other disciples followed in the boat, towing the net full of fish, for they were not far from shore, about a hundred yards. When they landed, they saw a fire of burning coals there with fish on it, and some bread. ...

"When they had finished eating, Jesus said to Simon Peter, 'Simon son of John, do you love me more than these?'

"'Yes, Lord,' he said, 'you know that I love you.'

"Jesus said, 'Feed my lambs.'

"Again Jesus said, 'Simon son of John, do you love me?'

"He answered, 'Yes, Lord, you know that I love you.'

"Jesus said, 'Take care of my sheep.'

"The third time he said to him, 'Simon son of John, do you love me?'

Meet me here as we sit on the seashore with Jesus and a broken man named Peter. After yesterday's gift of repentance, we have the privilege of being recommissioned just like Peter. Jesus brought Peter to a metaphorical altar of fire, where shame and guilt and regret were consumed. He brought him to a new commissioning where Peter took hold of Jesus' directives for his life. Everything in Peter's heart toward Jesus was reignited at this altar of fire.

When Peter met Jesus for the first time while he was fishing, the Lord invited this fisherman to follow Him and, from then on, fish for men. He had done that for the last three years and failed when it seemed like everything mattered. This broken man heard that the Lord was on the shoreline, clothed his nakedness, and swam to shore.

Jesus knew Peter would need a redo and a moment with His Savior, face-to-face. He prepared a catch of abundant provision, an intimate breakfast for His disciples, and a burning fire of remembrance.

Maybe you need that today.

Jesus has come and given you life in abundance (John 10:10). He has prepared a table before you, in the presence of your enemies, and meets you in lavish mercy and grace. He wants to take all that holds you back, that causes you to wrap your outer garments around you to cover yourself up before you meet with Him, and recommission you into the fullness and

 JULIE KING

abundance of His life, purposes, and plans. So come and sit around the fire, climb up on the altar, and let His words of life and recommissioning take hold of your heart.

He asks you, "Do you love Me?"

And again, "Do you love Me?"

And one more time, "Do you love Me?"

All three questions paralleled Peter's three denials. But this morning, the repetition is for your own soul. You can remind yourself of and declare your love for Him. And because of His cross, resurrection, and ascension, you have all barriers to forgiveness, redemption, and healing removed. What you bring to Jesus out of your repentance, He takes and restores for His glory and your healing.

It's at this fire on the shore of Tiberias that everything changed for Peter. He was able to move forward in God's calling on his life. He didn't need to return to fishing. He needed to follow God's command to go and catch people, feed them, and build His Church. Today, we ask the Lord to take us to the same new beginnings and do-over so we can walk into this season of revival with freedom from past wounds and failures and walk in abundant wholeness. It's at this altar of fire that we begin again.

You may find throughout your life that this passage of Scripture becomes foundational for you. I can testify that it has been for me, coming out of very dark and hard seasons throughout my 46 years with Jesus. Today, let it be a fresh encounter with the Lover of your soul at this altar of fire. The old has gone, and the new has come. Present yourself as a living sacrifice, holy and pleasing to the Lord. Take His clean, warm garments, and take the cold, wet ones off. Let Him feed you and love you and heal you as you stand by the fire He has prepared.

He who sees you loves you and will cause the flames of this fire to ignite your passion and His purposes from this day forward—just like He did for Peter. In the name of Jesus!

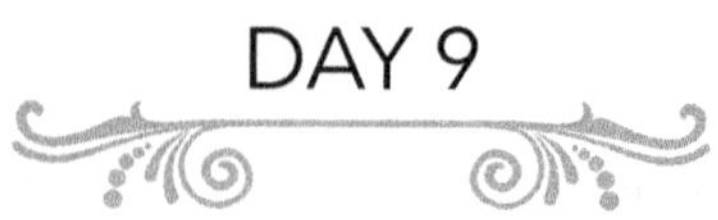

ENOUGH BREAD FOR YOU

*"From this time many of his disciples turned
back and no longer followed him."*
–John 6:66

My team and I hiked the jungle of the Himalayas to get to remote villages to tell people about Jesus. We covered 40 miles and at least a dozen villages in just four and a half days. As we were leaving the final village, a man sat on his little stoop to his house. He was completely deaf, so he could not hear about Jesus. Our team anointed his ears with oil, declared the name of Jesus over him, and prayed for his deaf ears to open. Upon being healed, he knew for the first time in his 80 years of the power and goodness and love of Jesus! It was a profound ending for our team and a brand new beginning for this man. We told him to tell everyone in his village about what Jesus had done for him.

This experience made me wrestle with the passage in John 6. How could some of Jesus' own disciples—those who had seen His miracles firsthand—turn away? What was it about His words that caused them to leave?

"Just as the living Father sent me and I live because of the Father,
so the one who feeds on me will live because of me. This is the
bread that came down from heaven. Your ancestors ate manna
and died, but whoever feeds on this bread will live forever."
—John 6:57–58

Upon hearing this, many of His disciples said, *"This is a hard teaching. Who can accept it (John 6:60)?"* The Greek word for "hard" here is *skleros*—not meaning difficult to understand but difficult to accept. Jesus wasn't just offering them material provision or comfort; He was asking for their whole lives. He was inviting them to feast on Him, the Bread of Life, and receive eternal life—but at the cost of surrendering everything else. And for many, that cost was too high.

Counting the Cost

I've seen this same struggle firsthand. When we tell Hindus about Jesus, they are often eager to accept the free gift of salvation. But when we tell them that Jesus is the only way—that they must forsake their other gods and worship Him alone—the weight of that decision is evident on their faces. They hesitate, counting the cost.

I believe that's what happened in John 6. The disciples weren't confused by Jesus' words; they were offended by them. Are You really asking me to give up my whole life? To trust that what You offer is greater than what I can see and touch? To let go of the things that bring me comfort and security?

"... the one who feeds on me will live because of me."
—John 6:57

Those who truly come to Jesus—who believe in Him, feed on Him—will find life. Not because they have achieved or earned it, but because Jesus freely gives them what He won at the cross.

The Test of Our Hearts

Today, we are watching the remaking of the American dream. Comfort, success, wealth—all these things compete for our attention and affection. I believe many will turn away from Jesus, just as they did in John 6, because He is calling us to feast on Him alone, not on the riches of this world.

Church, we could gain the whole world and lose our souls.

He is Enough

Beloved, today there is enough Bread for you. His life is enough. He longs to fill you with the fullness of Himself, to satisfy your deepest needs and desires.

Would you take a moment to listen to "At the Altar" by Elevation Rhythm? Our team worshiped to this song in weakness and frailty, laying ourselves down at the altar.

Today, will you do the same? Will you let Him feed you with the Bread that truly satisfies?

Revival is Here

Throughout history, every great revival has begun with a people willing to lay down their lives for the Bread of Life. When we hunger for Jesus above all else, He moves in power. The question remains: Will we feast on Him alone, or will we find the bread of the world? The choice we make in this hour will determine the depth of revival in our hearts and in our land. The Bread of Life is before us—come and eat.

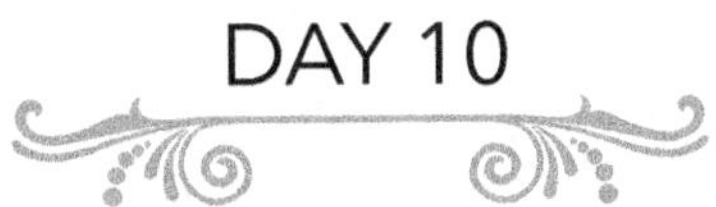

REVIVAL OF IDENTITY

*"I have been crucified with Christ and I no
longer live, but Christ lives in me.
The life I now live in the body, I live by faith in the Son of God,
who loved me and gave himself for me."
—Galatians 2:20*

As we pursue all of the facets of revival these 40 days, this passage of Scripture is foundational to both our understanding of revival and our identity as followers of Jesus. But I pray that, more than understanding, these words wash over you today like healing waters.

"I have been crucified with Christ … ."

This is the glorious truth and proclamation of who we are in Christ! All things of my sinful nature and dead self were crucified on the cross (Romans 6:6). We have been given a new nature, a new heart, and a new spirit (Ezekiel 36:26)! He took out our stony heart and put a heart of flesh that beats with the blood of Jesus (Hebrews 9:14). We have a new spiritual DNA written into our spiritual genetic code (John 1:12–13, 1 Peter 1:23). The old has gone, and the new has come (2 Corinthians 5:17). It's a done deal, past tense, and both final and effective!

The sparks of revival first begin when we, as followers of Jesus, choose to die to self, surrendering our own desires, pride, and sin to the cross. It's in the dying we find life and life in abundance.

> "The call to follow Christ was a call to die. The call to discipleship and obedience has always been one to deny self, to die to one's own ambitions and even self-preservation. Jesus has never changed the missionary call and conditions for following Him; indeed, the calling to anyone who would be His disciple is one of sacrifice and a willingness to lay down one's life." –Jerry Rankin, "Why Do Missionaries Go to Dangerous Places?"[4]

> *"... I no longer live, but Christ lives in me."*

Any true revival bursting forth from our lives is not the result of human striving but the unstoppable power of Christ living through us! When a heart is fully surrendered, the Holy Spirit ignites the Word of God like a blazing fire, bringing it to life in ways the world cannot ignore. It is in this divine overflow that the very presence of Jesus transforms individuals, ignites churches, awakens communities, and shakes nations.

To challenge your thinking even further, read another excerpt from Jerry's book: "... as long as we look on this life as home, we will be caught up in its values, seeking material comforts, worrying about our future, how our investments are doing, building homes, preparing for a comfortable retirement, seeking fulfillment in things of the world. ... There is something worth giving your life for, and yes, worth dying for."

> *"The life I now live in the body, I live by faith in the Son of God ... ."*

It's at the end of me that I truly live. It's when this sanctified life gives Jesus full rule and reign that revival fires are sparked in the places where we set our feet. Revival sustains when believers walk with Jesus in faith, trusting Him for strength and direction. Faith leads to boldness in sharing the gospel, praying what Jesus is praying for cities and nations, and renewed spiritual passion is set aflame. I no longer live, but Christ lives through me, and it's in this faith that my life is rooted and grounded and releases His Kingdom for His name's sake.

"… who loved me and gave himself for me."

The heartbeat of revival is experiencing and responding to the overwhelming love of Christ. His sacrificial love compels believers to love God wholeheartedly and serve others passionately. We model the crucified life of Christ when we love so sacrificially. Jesus' love for us cost Him everything. If we think we want our lives to matter for eternity, we have to wrestle with the reality that this kind of deep love for Jesus will most likely cost us everything.

A revived life, the life we pray for, will reflect Jesus' love, power, and faithfulness and result in an eternal impact on the world around us. How I long for this to be true of me!

I close with a gripping testimony from this beloved book I have been quoting throughout this devotional.

"At Karen Watson's funeral a friend reflected that they could tell something was happening in her life after each mission trip she went on. Finally, last year she resigned her job, sold her house, sold her car and gave away all her earthly possessions. She packed what was left in a duffle bag and headed for Iraq. Now, a year later, her friend reflected, all that was left was her duffle bag, her Bible and her devotion to Christ. Was it worth it? Karen had written in a letter [and] left it with her pastor, 'There are no regrets. My calling is to obedience, suffering is expected, and His glory is my reward.'" –Jerry Rankin, "Why Do Missionaries Go to Dangerous Places?"

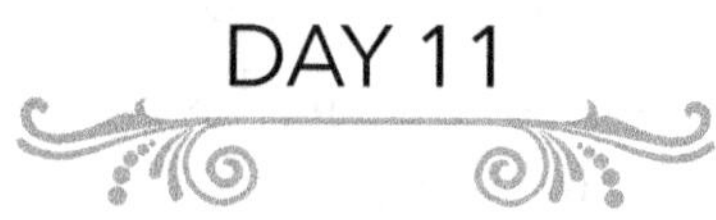

HUNGER FOR HOLINESS

*"Therefore, with minds that are alert and fully sober, set your hope
on the grace to be brought to you when Jesus Christ is revealed at his
coming. As obedient children, do not conform to the evil desires you had
when you lived in ignorance. But just as he who called you is holy, so
be holy in all you do; for it is written: 'Be holy, because I am holy.'"*
—1 Peter 1:13–16

*"'If you belonged to the world, it would love you as its own.
As it is, you do not belong to the world, but I have chosen you
out of the world. That is why the world hates you.'"*
—John 15:19

A friend relayed a call she had with some women church planters in South Asia. This team of women has planted thousands of churches and recently baptized 4,000 women. The state governor of one of the states in this particular country said his "gift" to women on this year's International Women's Day was that people caught sharing the gospel would not be persecuted. Instead of persecution, those caught sharing the gospel would simply be hanged.

Having just returned from this country and trekking 40 miles through their jungles to get to remote villages to share the gospel, this sobered me greatly. My sacrifice of worship to the Lord cost me some discomfort. However, these women's sacrifice of living for Jesus will most likely cost them their lives.

My soul wants comfortable Christianity, and my spirit, infused with the Spirit, propels me toward holiness and radical surrender. The struggle is real for us here in America.

I think back on this same type of trip when one of my teammates was giving herself cancer treatment injections and getting her pack on to go tell people about Jesus. I remember another woman who went with me in her first trimester of pregnancy and was so sick every morning. She, too, persevered so that entire villages could be reached with the gospel.

So how does this relate to holiness? The profundity of holiness is not about our behavior but our identity. It's what God sees when He looks at you. Holiness is simply being set apart for the purposes of God because of the devotion of Christ to His Father who lives in you. You have been set apart for the purposes of God in this hour, for this generation, and to shape history and nations. It's our high calling in Christ as priests who are wholly loved by the Lord. From this identity flow our pursuits, and everything we dedicate ourselves to is meant to bear fruit—for Him and for His glory.

I don't know the internal motivation of these women in South Asia, but I have to assume it's a passionate love for Jesus that compels them. When I gaze across the globe, there are countless testimonies of women laying their lives down to take the gospel forth. In many countries, the Church is being birthed and carried on the shoulders of women. But when I look at our nation, where only around 17% of churchgoers have a solid understanding of the Great Commission, my heart grieves. The anointing of God on women is not in proximity to the landscape but rather a response of God to the hunger in His people.

Holiness will never be about behavior modification in order to appear good. It's not about perfection before people. Holiness is about pure devotion to a life set apart, consecrated, unto the Lord.

"Oh, let us grasp this truth with both hands; let it never slip from us. Jesus Himself is our source of holiness! We are so eager to do something for Him—anything, as long as we do not have to change inside. God does not need what we can do; He wants what we are. He wants to make us a holy people. Let us not be anxious in this process. Allow Him to do the deep inner work of preparation. Jesus lived thirty years of sinless purity before He did one work of power! His goal was not to do some great work but to please the Father with a holy life." –Francis Frangipane, "Holiness, Truth and the Presence of God"[5]

Beloved, I exhort you as I look in the mirror at myself. Our holiness is our identity, but it is also the pursuit of our lives that results in radical exploits for God. He is not asking for our holy behavior without consecration that just results in religion. He is asking for the intimacy of our lives wrapped in His life, anchored in who Christ is in us, living out His life in this world. The cost to us, therefore, is wrapped in the person of Jesus and His sacrifice, and it is sealed and marked by His blood and by His Spirit. We, therefore, exude holiness from our innermost being so that the world takes notice and Jesus receives the love of our whole surrendered life, even unto death.

Lord, create in me an insatiable desire for holiness. Do this in me so that my whole life is consecrated to You and Your purposes!

HOLY SPIRIT: THE BREATH OF REVIVAL

*"'I have much more to say to you, more than you can now bear. But when he, the Spirit of truth, comes, he will guide you into all the truth. He will not speak on his own; he will speak only what he hears, **and he will tell you what is yet to come**. He will glorify me because it is from me that he will receive **what he will make known to you**. All that belongs to the Father is mine. That is why I said the Spirit will receive from me what he will make known to you.'*

"Jesus went on to say, 'In a little while you will see me no more, and then after a little while you will see me.'"
–John 16:12–16, emphasis added

I dreamt that I was at a large gathering of people around a meal. It was quite chaotic, and the table was on a hill that was sloping downward. I was trying to get everyone seated, and I remember in the prayer crying out in deep longing for Jesus to come back. I remember an eagerness to get others to have the same longing for the return of Jesus, but so many were so distracted.

These days feel like such critical days that we, as a Church, have an opportunity to seize. We still have freedom to move about and preach the gospel, but the invitation to sit back and relish in these days of peace and prosperity is quite real. This is the Scripture that continually resounds my heart and mind: *"As long as it is day, we must do the works of him who sent me. Night is coming, when no one can work (John 9:4)."*

Jesus knew the tension of what was soon coming, and yet His disciples were somewhat clueless. He gave them indication of what He was about to suffer, but they didn't grasp the severity of it. *"They kept asking, 'What does he mean by "a little while"? We don't understand what he is saying (John 16:18).'"* I don't want to be caught in a space of bewilderment or cluelessness for this time in which we are living. The Spirit of truth will bring clarity and revelation and deposit eternity in our hearts.

The Spirit of Jesus who lives actively inside of us will tell and is telling us what is to come. He is making known to us the times and the seasons to which we are living, and I believe it's time to tune our ears and open His Word because He isn't silent in these very crucial and urgent days. There are millions of Christians all over the world who carry the death, burial, and resurrection of Jesus inside of them. If these millions of Christ followers lived with the cry of Maranatha on their lips and their feet shod with the gospel of peace, the ends of the Earth could be reached with the gospel.

The Holy Spirit is not a passive bystander. He longs to reveal Jesus through your life. This Counselor of truth and Revealer of mysteries has much to say to us if we will listen.

> Are we willing to listen?
> Are we willing to adjust to what He is speaking and showing us?
> Are we cooperating with God's redemptive plan for the world?

I find this quote quite compelling:

> "We may not always agree when it comes to certain issues, be they doctrinal, political, or social. However, we do agree on the gospel, and we are all striving to be led by the Holy Spirit in righteousness and holiness. That must unite us together, and it must unite us now! We cannot wait until ten minutes before inspection to clean up our act. We must be about the Father's gospel business today and every day until our Savior returns to take us to be with Him." –Amir Tsarfati, "Has the Tribulation Begun?"[6]

The Holy Spirit will pioneer and bring forth revival. It's what He's done since the book of Acts so that the ends of the Earth can know Jesus. His plan will be fulfilled, no question about it. Within that reality, every single Christ follower has a role in the fulfillment of God's redemptive plan for the world. His choice is you and me. Revival will come with the breath of God breathing new life into people, which overflows into families, cities, and nations. But the question I want you to wrestle with deeply is, what part will you have in this co-mission with God? We don't get to just be consumers in the economy of God. It's never what Jesus modeled when He gave His whole life, unto death, for the salvation of the world.

What is the Spirit of God making known to you in this season? What is He challenging you to step into for the sake of all of eternity? My challenge for those of you longing to see revival is this: Will you ask the Holy Spirit to make you a revivalist and to go into all the world and preach the gospel? He will sort out all of the details as you simply make yourself available!

LIVING WITH THE END IN MIND

"He said to them: 'It is not for you to know the times or dates the Father has set by his own authority. But you will receive power when the Holy Spirit comes on you; and you will be my witnesses in Jerusalem, and in all Judea and Samaria, and to the ends of the earth.'

"After he said this, he was taken up before their very eyes, and a cloud hid him from their sight. They were looking intently up into the sky as he was going, when suddenly two men dressed in white stood beside them. 'Men of Galilee,' they said, 'why do you stand here looking into the sky? This same Jesus, who has been taken from you into heaven, will come back in the same way you have seen him go into heaven.'

"Then the apostles returned to Jerusalem from the hill called the Mount of Olives, a Sabbath day's walk from the city."
—Acts 1:7-12

We've been sourced with the promised Holy Spirit—our power source for life and ministry. We are walking on the roadmap for life, to the ends of the Earth, in the fullness of all Jesus promised us. But the most beautiful promise we fix our eyes on is this: *"This same Jesus, who has been taken from you into heaven, will come back in the same way you have seen him go into heaven (Acts 1:11b)."* He's coming back for His Bride! And it is unto this end that the reason for our perseverance in the gospel and our cry for revival finds its focus.

Jesus was taken up in a cloud that is understood to be a *Shekinah* glory of God's presence. We see it in both the Old and New Testaments. He did not disappear before them, but they were able to see Him standing with them and then go away like He said He would do. This was to fulfill His words in John 16:7, ESV: *"Nevertheless, I tell you the truth: it is to your advantage that I go away, for if I do not go away, the Helper will not come to you. But if I go, I will send him to you."* Jesus wanted His followers to know this was the departure they had been waiting for!

Two angels in white stood beside these onlookers, redirecting their gaze to the obedience of their hearts, asking them why they were just standing there. It was time to return to Jerusalem like Jesus had commanded them to do. These ones had a sure directive—the ends of the Earth—but they stood there pondering and looking into the sky. It was time for their radical obedience as the Spirit was on His way now that Jesus had gone. It was time to go!

This same Jesus—who was the same throughout the gospels; unchanging in His promise and power; faithful to His word; the same yesterday, today, and forever—was now seated at the right hand of the Father! And when the Father will tell His Son that it is time to go and get His Bride, He will come back for us. But first, these followers of Jesus had to receive all they needed through the Spirit of Christ, who longed to now reside inside of them.

The angels told them, *"This same Jesus, who has been taken from you into heaven, will come back in the same way you have seen him go into heaven."*

I have set my sights on this reality. It is not so I can sit back and put my feet up and wait to be rescued. The gospel will be preached throughout the world during the tribulation. There are three main ways Revelation points to the expansion of the gospel: the 144,000 witnesses, the two witnesses (prophets), and the angels that circle the globe. But for those of us awaiting the rapture of the Church, it is with urgency that we share the gospel so that those we love will not be left behind to endure the seven-year tribulation period. It is my desire and prayer that I tell as many people as possible, in as many nations as possible, of the salvation of Jesus.

> "The disciples didn't know how long it would be before He would return, but they lived as if it was imminent. Again, that word means that He could come at any time. So, after a Holy Spirit boost at Pentecost, these men jumped fully into their roles as spreaders of the gospel. For all but one of them, it would cost their lives—a price they willingly paid.

> "What was so different about them that they could be that gung-ho about spreading Jesus' message of salvation? Was it that they had seen the Lord? That may be part of it. But there are plenty of examples of believers who have given their lives for the gospel who never laid their physical eyes on the Savior. … Remember, they were just a bunch of fishermen, blue-collar workers, and a tax collector. What made the difference for them is that they committed to carrying out the mission of Christ no matter the cost. How can we, living in this world of contradiction, also keep our eyes on the eternal rather than the temporal? The answer to that question is where we find the 'So what?' of what appears to be our soon-coming departure." –Amir Tsarfati, "Has the Tribulation Begun?"[7]

Our King Jesus is coming back for His Bride. As the eschatological clock seems to be ticking quickly, where are your sights? Are you navel-gazing, wondering how to build up your temporal reserves, ensure your comfort, and accomplish your bucket list? Are you getting the Word of God deep inside of you so you don't fall away from the faith in these challenging days? Would you count the cost and, on your face before Jesus, say to Him, "I am willing; send me." This is between you and Jesus. This hour we find ourselves in is our hour to lay it all down and spend our remaining days being poured out for the sake of the gospel!

"The Spirit and the bride say, 'Come!' And let the one who hears say, 'Come!' Let the one who is thirsty come; and let the one who wishes take the free gift of the water of life. ...

"He who testifies to these things says, 'Yes, I am coming soon.'

"Amen. Come, Lord Jesus.

"The grace of the Lord Jesus be with God's people. Amen."
—Revelation 22:17, 20-21

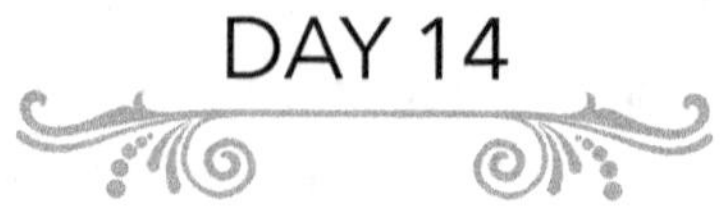

AT HIS FEET

"When Mary reached the place where Jesus was and saw him, she fell at his feet and said, 'Lord, if you had been here, my brother would not have died.'"
—John 11:32

"She had a sister called Mary, who sat at the Lord's feet listening to what he said."
—Luke 10:39

"Then Mary took about a pint of pure nard, an expensive perfume; she poured it on Jesus' feet and wiped his feet with her hair. And the house was filled with the fragrance of the perfume."
—John 12:3

I have pondered something for weeks as I paralleled these three passages of Scripture together. Mary was identified by her sitting at the feet of Jesus. This is where she is often found and a most beautiful descriptor of her life.

In desperation, she surrendered at the feet of Jesus.
In quietness and teachability, she sat at His feet.
In worship, she poured it all out on His feet.

Jesus invited Mary to sit at His feet, and today He is inviting you to do the same.

Women were not permitted in those days to learn at the feet of rabbis, and they certainly were not permitted to let their hair down and wash the feet of a man during a meal. Mary lived with a heart set apart for Jesus. Culture would not limit her expression or worship of the One she loved. There weren't immovable barriers for Mary. When Jesus pulled her to Himself, she came. When faced with death and grief, she submitted to His lordship over her life and circumstances. Does my love for Jesus look like this? If a biography were written of my life, would it say, "She was always found at the feet of Jesus"?

> "You must sit at His feet, or you will never anoint them!
> He must pour His Divine teaching into you, or you will
> never pour out a precious ointment upon Him!" –Charles
> Spurgeon

Nothing was too costly for Mary to pour out on Jesus; her tears, her time, and her treasure all belonged to Jesus. They belonged to Him because she belonged to Him. And in the falling down at His feet, the sitting at His feet, or the bending low to anoint His feet, her heart, too, bent low. She held one common position—humble surrender at the feet of Jesus. He held the rightful place in her heart. He held a place no other deserved.

> *"'... but few things are needed—or indeed only one.*
> *Mary has chosen what is better, and it will not be taken away from her.'"*
> *–Luke 10:42*

Jesus was Lord in Mary's life. He was her one thing. He was the only thing that mattered. And in every different place, the desire in Mary remained the same: to sit at the feet of Jesus, to worship and weep there. Every context drove Mary to the same end—at His feet.

Feet that would hold the weight of His broken body on
the cross.
Feet that would willingly walk to Jerusalem to face the
end of His life on Earth.
Feet that would walk a cross on His bloodied back to "the
place of the skull."
Feet that would walk into towns that refused to believe
He was the Son of God.
Feet that would leave the streets of Heaven for the dirt
roads of Earth.
Feet that would walk out of a grave and into your life to
make His home in you.

I want the simplicity of adoration Mary had for Jesus. He was her everything—her very treasure. Jesus loved and embraced and taught Mary so intimately that going to the feet of Jesus was her rightful response. So much healing and belonging took place at the feet of Jesus for Mary. Let us find our dwelling place this month at the feet of Jesus.

Let me close with the questions I am compelled to personally ask the Lord after pondering these testimonies of Mary's devotion, worship, and surrender.

Do I go to the feet of Jesus before I go and do ministry?
Do I run from thing to thing, like Martha, doing good
things but not the best thing?
When I am grieving or disillusioned, do I run to the feet
of my friend or husband before I go to the feet of Jesus?
Do all of my treasures get poured out on the feet of Jesus
or the feet of the world?
Do I live at His feet or just go there from time to time?

Mary received what she needed at His feet. Then, He helped her to get up and go. She walked to Lazarus' tomb with Jesus to witness a miracle. She got up from sitting and anointing His feet in order to face the brutality of the cross. Her positioning at His feet prepared her for what God was about to do. Take hold of that truth in this month of preparation. This is why we return to our first love. There will be something God will prepare in you for what is to come. But first, we go to His feet.

HEALED AND RESTORED

"When one of the Pharisees invited Jesus to have dinner with him, he went to the Pharisee's house and reclined at the table. A woman in that town who lived a sinful life learned that Jesus was eating at the Pharisee's house, so she came there with an alabaster jar of perfume. As she stood behind him at his feet weeping, she began to wet his feet with her tears. Then she wiped them with her hair, kissed them and poured perfume on them. …

"Then he turned toward the woman and said to Simon, 'Do you see this woman? I came into your house. You did not give me any water for my feet, but she wet my feet with her tears and wiped them with her hair. You did not give me a kiss, but this woman, from the time I entered, has not stopped kissing my feet. You did not put oil on my head, but she has poured perfume on my feet. Therefore, I tell you, her many sins have been forgiven—as her great love has shown. But whoever has been forgiven little loves little.'

"Then Jesus said to her, 'Your sins are forgiven.'

"The other guests began to say among themselves, 'Who is this who even forgives sins?'

"Jesus said to the woman, 'Your faith has saved you; go in peace.'"
–Luke 7:36–38, 44–50

As we journey together throughout these 40 days of pursuing revival, I don't want us to miss the gift of repentance as we return to the Lord. There is something so beautiful and outrageous about godly repentance found in this passage.

Normally I will read this passage through the eyes of the woman, longing to bring her best gift to Jesus and pour it all on Him. In fact, this is one of my favorite passages to motivate my mission teams as we head into the field for ministry. But as I reread this, I saw something different. If you look at her broken and contrite spirit, she is receiving something from the Lord in her repentance. Jesus is washing her clean, forgiving her of her sin, shame, and guilt. He is so tender toward her, not condemning her nor preaching to her about the degree of her sin. Instead, He removes all of the degrading shame and sin. He recognizes her faith and repentance and tells her three things:

"'Your sins are forgiven.'"

"'Your faith has saved you … .'"

"'… go in peace.'"

She didn't ask for any of these three gifts. But Jesus knew exactly what she needed in order to be free. Essentially, she came to love Jesus and worship Him, but Jesus did something even greater so she could be free. What a glorious exchange.

Jesus invites us to an encounter with Him afresh. There are places in our lives and in our hearts that are burdened with so many things. The cares of the world can choke out our love for Jesus. We search high and low for temporal things to give us momentary relief, and we just pile on the regrets, idols, baggage, and entanglements. Jesus wants us to be free. Our freedom is what He paid for with His whole life. If we will just come to Him and own what we need to own as the Holy Spirit brings it into the light, He will say the same things He said to this worshiping woman: *"'Your sins are forgiven. … Your faith has saved you; go in peace.'"*

It's time to be free so your heart can draw near to Jesus. He has so much to show you.

Jesus, shepherd us and lead us beside quiet waters where You restore our souls. I pray for the spirit of repentance to fall upon each one of us so that we may receive the gift of freedom You died to give us. Show us, in the secret place, where we need to repent of things hidden in darkness or below the surface of our lives that need to be brought into the light. And as we sit at Your feet like the woman in this passage, may we love and worship You as You minister and receive each one of us. This is a gift and an opportunity to repent and return. Show us, Holy Spirit, what those areas are today so we can receive a deeper understanding of Your unfathomable love, grace, and mercy. In the name of Jesus, amen.

DAY 16

THE DOOR OF REVIVAL

"I slept but my heart was awake. Listen! My beloved is knocking:
'Open to me, my sister, my darling, my dove, my flawless one. My head
is drenched with dew, my hair with the dampness of the night.'"
—Song of Solomon 5:2

"'Be dressed ready for service and keep your lamps burning, like servants
waiting for their master to return from a wedding banquet, so that when
he comes and knocks they can immediately open the door for him. It will
be good for those servants whose master finds them watching when he
comes. Truly I tell you, he will dress himself to serve, will have them recline
at the table and will come and wait on them. It will be good for those
servants whose master finds them ready, even if he comes in the middle
of the night or toward daybreak. … You also must be ready, because
the Son of Man will come at an hour when you do not expect him.'"
—Luke 12:35–38, 40

"'Here I am! I stand at the door and knock. If anyone hears my voice and
opens the door, I will come in and eat with that person, and they with me.'"
—Revelation 3:20

*J*esus stands at the door of the world, knocking. He stands at the door of the Church, knocking. He stands at the door of global chaos, knocking. He stands at the door of your life, knocking. The birth pangs are allowing us to hear His knocking on another level if our spiritual ears are tuned in. In fact, it's in the shaking that His presence is more and more known to us; His voice is more and more dear to us; and the thought of keeping Him behind closed doors creates eager longing to swing wide the door so that the King of glory may come in.

I want to take you on a journey of subsequent doors through all three passages of Scripture: Song of Solomon, the words of Jesus in Luke, and the angel's record of the invitation to the Church of Laodicea. These represent three doors that Jesus is standing behind, and on the other side are three brides, all representative of the Church.

He Stands at Your Door as Your Beloved

We have a sleepy maiden who is awakened by the voice of her beloved. He is eager to be with her and is waiting so long that dew fills his hair. Perhaps he came unexpectedly. From the sounds of it, she's just as eager for his intimacy and embrace. But for some reason, the door is locked, and he can't get in his own house. Somehow, there's a barrier between them. Both are longing for one another, but something keeps them separated. He knocks. When she finally goes to let him in, she can't find him anywhere (Song of Solomon 5:6).

Place yourself in this picture with Jesus on the other side of the door. What is blocking you from an intimate encounter with Him? Is it the exhaustion of working for the Lord? Religious duties? A love affair with another? The noises of the world that keep you from hearing His hand knocking?

Search me, oh God, and remove any barriers. Unlock the door. I want to run into Your embrace.

JULIE KING

He Stands at the Door as the Master of the House

Jesus tells a parable about a master returning to find his servants watching and ready for him. Their ears are listening for his arrival. When he knocks, they are ready to open the door for him. The lights are on. Anticipation is in the air; in fact, the atmosphere is thick with excitement! Can you imagine your racing heart at the sound of his knock?

In preparation for that day, is there anything that is stealing your focus? Is your house in order? Will your neighbors know where you have gone? Will they go with you? Are your lamps filled with oil? Will He find you busy about His business or distracted and frantic?

Search my heart, Lord. Clean the rooms of my heart so that this home, the place You reside, is clean and ready. Find the porch light on in my life.

He Stands at the Door as Savior

To the sinner and the saint, His invitation is the same. He wants to dine with us. He wants to have a meaningful conversation and an intimate relationship. For some reason, we find Jesus in this passage once again on the other side of the door.

I love the commentary from David Guzik on this passage: "This statement of Jesus expressed a profound mystery. Why did Jesus stand outside the door? Why did He knock? Why did He wait until someone opens the door? He had every right to break down the door, or enter some other way on His own accord, but He didn't. The sovereign, omnipotent Jesus lowered Himself to work out His eternal plan by wooing the cooperation of the human heart."

It's imperative to open the door when we first hear His voice. Our listening ears tell our brain to run to the door and throw it wide open. When we listen to His voice, we can be saved from lukewarmness and move to a passionate love relationship with Jesus.

Picture this door of your life, oh saint. As Jesus stands at the door of your life, what is He calling to you that you need to hear? What has He come to awaken in you, just like He did at the doors in the other two passages of Scripture? He comes as a Lover and Savior over and over again. But today, this door is a door that, in this season, is in preparation for His return. He stands at it to bring you something imperative for the road ahead.

Jesus, open our spiritual ears to hear Your words that You are calling to us. Whatever door is shut between us, will You knock loud and give us the faith to swing it wide open so You can walk right through? What have You come to bring us to feast on together?

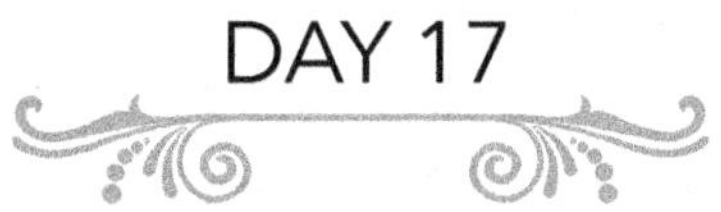

SALTED WITH FIRE

"'Everyone will be salted with fire.'"
–Mark 9:49

We are continuing our 40-day pursuit of revival, pursuing Jesus with even greater intentionality and focus. I pray that your heart has done some 180-degree turns with the Lord again and again this season. I pray that broken places have been healed and restored. I pray that you are experiencing your own personal revival so that you can carry forth the fires of revival in this significant moment in His story. When I read this Scripture months ago, it spoke to me of the many things that we must take hold of as we traverse this time. Lord, salt us with fire for the days in which we are living!

Jesus had been teaching in Mark 9 about the seriousness of sin, calling His followers to carefully consider the consecration of a pure and faithful life. In this verse, Jesus uses powerful metaphors—salt and fire—to illustrate how God refines and purifies us.

In ancient times, salt was used to preserve, purify, and sustain life. In the Old Testament, salt was symbolic of covenant faithfulness (Leviticus 2:13). Christ is continually sustaining us and purifying us, making us ready for the coming of Jesus. He sets us apart for His purposes in the Earth and works with you to preserve the spiritual health of your life. All the while, you are being sanctified through and through, being made more like Jesus.

Fire often represents purification (Malachi 3:2–3) or testing (1 Peter 1:7) in Scripture. As fire refines metal by removing impurities, God uses trials to refine our faith. Each one of us can list the fires we have walked through or are walking through. I would say the Church in America is in the fire, and we have a choice to make: How will we choose to come forth?

We don't get to go through life without enduring trials. They are a part of the human experience. We will all be salted with fire, most likely again and again. But what is brought forth is a purity and holiness, refining and strengthening in the Lord and the faith we place in Him.

Jesus wants the perpetual, addictive, recurring sin to be purged out of us. He's longing for a people who are Holy in heart and conduct just as much as they are in identity. We bear the holiness of Christ, so the inside and outside need to come together in perfect alignment.

Therefore, our prayer becomes, "Lord Jesus, circumcise my heart, crucify my flesh, and consecrate every part of my life unto holiness." Repentance has played a key role in our returning to Him. I love what Dr. Rob Reimer writes regarding this sacred turning:

> "Repentance is returning to the safety of God's house. This is why God calls us to follow Him, and when we wander, He calls us to repent. He is calling us back home, into His presence. It isn't with judgment that He calls us home; it is with the tender heart of love." –Dr. Rob Reimer, "The Tenderness of Jesus"

There is safety in the shadow of the Almighty. Jesus is the fourth man in the fire with us. He will be faithful when we are faithless. We can bank our lives on all of these truths. But will He find faith when He comes to take you home? Jesus asks us even today, *"... when the Son of Man comes, will he find faith on the earth (Luke 18:8)?"*

Perhaps my prayer articulates the desire of your own heart:

Lord, will You so consecrate my life that its saltiness attracts others to desire the purity and holiness of Jesus? Let the fire of holiness burn deep in my bones. Whatever and whoever is not of You, remove so that the sacred places of my heart hold affection for the One my heart so desires. Let the love for my first love burn even hotter; revive me once again. Jesus, remove the foxes in my vineyard that bring destruction and devastation. Keep my eyes in laser-focused vision on the One my heart adores. May I come out of this year with fresh vision, passion, fire, and love for You, Jesus. Today, I cry out to You. Consecrate me afresh and salt me with fire!

"May God himself, the God of peace, sanctify you through and through. May your whole spirit, soul and body be kept blameless at the coming of our Lord Jesus Christ."
—1 Thessalonians 5:23

DAY 18

RESET, REMEMBER, RETURN

"'To the angel (divine messenger) of the church in Ephesus write:

"'These are the words of the One who holds [firmly] the seven stars [which are the angels or messengers of the seven churches] in His right hand, the One who walks among the seven golden lampstands (the seven churches):

"''I know your deeds and your toil, and your patient endurance, and that you cannot tolerate those who are evil, and have tested and critically appraised those who call themselves apostles (special messengers, personally chosen representatives, of Christ), and [in fact] are not, and have found them to be liars and impostors; and [I know that] you [who believe] are enduring patiently and are bearing up for My name's sake, and that you have not grown weary [of being faithful to the truth]. But I have this [charge] against you, that you have left your first love [you have lost the depth of love that you first had for Me]. So remember the heights from which you have fallen, and repent [change your inner self—your old way of thinking, your sinful behavior—seek God's will] and do the works you did at first [when you first knew Me]; otherwise, I will visit you and remove your lampstand (the church, its impact) from its place—unless you repent."''
—Revelation 2:1–5, AMP

ime seems to go faster and faster! But we have not lost sight of what we are holding on to: revival. We are dedicating this time to pursuing God's heart for the world and the part we play. He said in the last days that the love of many would grow cold. We seek to guard our hearts from this reality. We long to be people revived by the very breath of God and living out the fires of revival every place our feet tread. So, this morning, pause, slow down, and reset for the remaining days of this journey.

This is the time that we let religion and legalism fall to the ground. This is a time of doing a 180-degree turn in the places of our hearts that need repentance and returning. Jesus holds you securely in this process and will be faithful, by His Spirit, to bring counsel and revelation. He will bring to the surface what must turn in repentance and affection toward Jesus.

In spite of all the good the things the Church in Ephesus did, Jesus looked at them and said, """*... you have left your first love (Revelation 2:4, AMP).*""" They did not lose their first love—He is not going anywhere. He remains faithful even in our faithlessness. Everything looked good on the outside, but their hearts were drifting.

> **Remember** where you came from, your life before salvation.
> **Remember** the thrill of love when you found Jesus.
> **Remember** all He did on the cross for you.
> **Remember** the love birthed in you for Jesus and for one another.

Let's rediscover the depth of love we first felt for Jesus, whose love remains steadfast. Often, our love shifts under the weight of religion, burdens, and deferred hope; our souls get battered and bruised. Join me and other women these 40 days as we revisit our love affair with Jesus.

Retreat into the secret place where it's just you and Him. There, He will reveal the repentance needed for you to return to that original connection.

> **Return** to the place where your love and heart can be renewed.
> **Return** to the place where your fire first began.
> **Return** to the place where He wants to launch you again into a deep, passionate love for Him.

I want to remind you of a profound truth:

"Who shall separate us from the love of Christ? Shall trouble or hardship or persecution or famine or nakedness or danger or sword? As it is written: 'For your sake we face death all day long; we are considered as sheep to be slaughtered.' No, in all these things we are more than conquerors through him who loved us. For I am convinced that neither death nor life, neither angels nor demons, neither the present nor the future, nor any powers, neither height nor depth, nor anything else in all creation, will be able to separate us from the love of God that is in Christ Jesus our Lord."
—Romans 8:35–39

Let us return to that love!

Jesus, we come face down, hands wide open to receive all You have for us in the revival of our own hearts. We consecrate the remainder of these 40 days to you and ask You to protect them. Take us back to where intimacy was born, where our love for You first burned. Free us from religion's chains that say we must earn Your love. Set us free to run with You, anchored in deep, passionate love. Help us remember, repent, and return. May this be a normal rhythm in our lives. We want to be all in with You and encounter the Lover of our souls afresh. In Jesus' merciful name, amen.

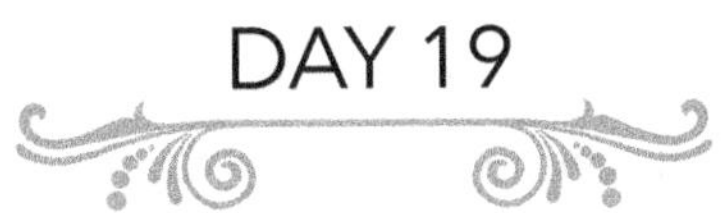

FROM HEAVEN TO EARTH

"… your kingdom come, your will be done, on earth as it is in heaven."
—Matthew 6:10

One of my favorite books these last few years is Amir Tsarfati's book called "Has the Tribulation Begun?" It has given me a firm biblical foundation on eschatology and the rapture of the Church. There will come a time when the wrath of God will be poured on the wicked and on Israel. Many will come to Christ during those seven years, and the eyes of the Jewish people will be opened to salvation in Christ. We are not living in those days yet. In fact, I would dare to say that in these days of wars and rumors of war, we are seeing the goodness and glory of God being poured out across the Earth. The news would not say this, but being knee-deep in the nations, I can attest to the wind of the Spirit, the fire of revival, and the saving grace of Jesus covering the Earth.

I returned recently from a suffering and decimated Latin American country. Scores of people ran to Jesus for salvation! It was glorious, to put it mildly. My co-leader and I had the absolute honor to spend a couple of hours with 28 prostitutes and their children. We opened the Word with them, and all 28 gave their lives to Jesus. Many of these women suffer abuse, sickness, hopelessness, disease, and despair. But Jesus came that day and reached out His nail-pierced hands and drew them to Himself.

Heaven touched Earth that day in this little village town, and women were saved, healed, and delivered!

> "In Matthew 6:10, Jesus instructs His disciples to decree these words in prayer: 'Your kingdom come. Your will be done, *on earth as it is in heaven.*' This is a revival prayer! For the past 2,000 years, the church has been praying for the kingdom of heaven—the rule and reign of God—to be established and manifested on earth. In essence, we have been praying for Revival with a capital 'R.' But this is also a prayer for reformation. It's not only for us individually or for our families; it's a prayer for our nations." –Ché Ahn, "Blueprints for Transformation"[8]

As we press into the heart of revival, may the prayer and declaration of Matthew 6:10 be the most familiar words on our tongue. As we seek to align our hearts with God's purposes now, in this crucial hour, let's invite His rule, reign, and manifest presence into our lives, communities, and nations.

Here's how we take hold of Matthew 6:10:

It Welcomes God's Sovereignty

Praying this verse is a declaration of surrender to God's rule. Revival begins when people lay down their own agendas and invite God's authority to be established, personally and corporately.

It Establishes Heaven's Priorities on Earth

Revival is a manifestation of Heaven touching Earth, mirroring God's love, justice, healing, and power. When we pray "on Earth as it is in Heaven," we're asking God to make our reality reflect His.

It Positions Us for Obedience

This prayer shapes our posture to not only desire God's will but to live it. Revival spreads through yielded hearts that say, "Yes," to His purposes, no matter the cost.

It Stirs Expectation and Faith

Praying Matthew 6:10 cultivates expectancy for supernatural transformation. It's a faith-filled request that believes God wants to move and will move when we invite Him.

It Unifies the Church Around God's Mission

True revival often comes when believers pray in unity for God's will, not their own. This prayer centers us around a shared cry, "Lord, let Your Kingdom come here—now."

In essence, Matthew 6:10 is a revival prayer at its core. It is a call for divine interruption, for God's rule to overtake human systems, and for His presence to bring life where there has been death.

To apply this even more, I want to give you a guided prayer you can use and integrate into your intercession for revival. Paste it in your journal to refer back to again and again.

Prayer Guide: "Your Kingdom Come, Your Will Be Done" (Matthew 6:10).

Your Kingdom Come: Welcome God's Reign

Pray:
- Lord, we invite Your Kingdom rule into every area of our lives—our hearts, our homes, our churches, and our cities.
- We ask You to dismantle every competing kingdom—our pride, our control, our agendas.
- Reign in our thoughts, words, and actions. Be enthroned where You belong.

Pause and Reflect:
- Ask the Holy Spirit: Where have I been building my own kingdom instead of Yours?

Your Will be Done: Surrender to His Will

Pray:
- Father, we surrender to Your perfect will. Teach us to love what You love and hate what You hate.
- We confess that we often chase comfort over calling. Align our desires with Yours.
- Let obedience rise in our hearts—even before we understand.

Declaration:
- Pray again: Not my will, but Yours be done—whatever the cost, wherever You lead.

Pray:

- Bring Heaven's atmosphere to Earth—purity, peace, healing, justice, power, and presence.
- Let revival fire fall—where the sick are healed, the lost are saved, and the bound are set free.
- Awaken Your Church, Lord. Make us carriers of Your glory and vessels of Your Spirit.

Intercede for Others:

- Pray for your family, church, city, and nation, asking God to make them places where Heaven touches Earth.

Listen and Respond

Quiet yourself and ask:

- Holy Spirit, how are You inviting me to partner with Heaven today?
- Is there someone You want me to pray for, serve, or encourage?

Write down what you hear; then take action.

Closing Prayer:

Father, we thank You that revival is initiated by You and continues through surrendered hearts. We give our yes to Your kingdom and yes to Your will. Let Your presence flood our lives and our land. Make us faithful in prayer, bold in love, and quick to obey. In Jesus' name, amen.

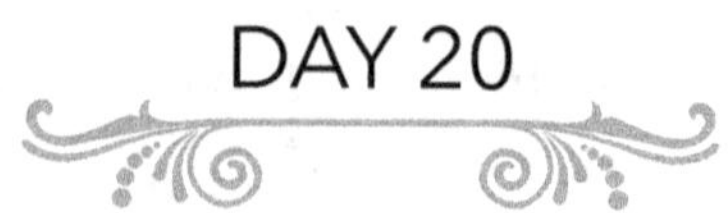

SET CAPTIVES FREE

"The Lord said, 'I have indeed seen the misery of my people in Egypt. I have heard them crying out because of their slave drivers, and I am concerned about their suffering. So I have come down to rescue them from the hand of the Egyptians and to bring them up out of that land into a good and spacious land, a land flowing with milk and honey— the home of the Canaanites, Hittites, Amorites, Perizzites, Hivites and Jebusites. And now the cry of the Israelites has reached me, and I have seen the way the Egyptians are oppressing them. So now, go. I am sending you to Pharaoh to bring my people the Israelites out of Egypt.'"
—Exodus 3:7–10

I am writing this devotional from a very raw place. I just experienced a level of suffering and oppression my head and heart had no category for. Deep in a desert in South Asia exist 16,000 "brick land" villages. They are owned and run by slave owners and inhabited primarily by both Hindu and Christian slaves. For generations, these slaves have made bricks in order to pay down the past debts of their families. They work every day, in the heat, with no shade trees, making bricks with straw and mud. They must make 1,600 bricks a day for just $3.

As I walked through one village trying to process the mercy of God in such a place, I anchored my heart in the fact that God never leaves them nor forsakes them. I wonder, though, if they have stopped crying out for deliverance, knowing this is their plight until their debt is paid off one day, many generations from now.

God heard the cries of His people in Egypt. He saw, He heard, He knew their misery and pain. And He sent a rescuer to go and bring His deliverance to His people. Moses surely didn't feel like he was qualified to do what God had assigned him to do. After 40 years in Midian as a shepherd, Moses met the assignment from God with great question and objection. However, God would be faithful to His people and send someone to set them free.

> *"I love the Lord, for he heard my voice; he heard my cry for mercy. Because he turned his ear to me, I will call on him as long as I live. The cords of death entangled me, the anguish of the grave came over me; I was overcome by distress and sorrow. Then I called on the name of the Lord: 'Lord, save me!'"*
> *—Psalm 116:1–4*

As I walked and processed this slavery and oppression, I was confronted with this very truth: the Rescuer for all of mankind lives inside you and me. It is our mandate to set captives free and not turn a deaf ear to the groaning of nations awaiting sons and daughters to take their place in this historic moment.

> *"The whole creation waits breathless with anticipation for the revelation of God's sons and daughters."*
> *—Romans 8:19, CEB*

The prophetic anointing Isaiah spoke of Jesus is our mandate, Church. The brick land villages are a picture of the world needing to encounter the lifesaving, debt-paying power of Jesus. I think what struck me so deeply is that we have an opportunity to do what we can do with the resources God has given us in America to help pay the debt of these families and set them free. It mirrors the cross so profoundly. We can partner with organizations and pay a family's debt so they can be released from slavery.

On an even greater level, it is time, Church, to make the last commandment of Christ in Matthew 28:18–20 our first and highest priority in this hour. Without Christ, people are caught in darkness, debt, and spiritual slavery they cannot get out of on their own. They need a Rescuer and Redeemer. They need the hope of eternal life and the hope of new life only Jesus can bring. I had one woman say to me, "Well, I don't have that gift," regarding telling people about Jesus. It's not a gift; it's a commandment from the mouth of Jesus that we either heed or ignore.

I want to declare your identity to you today:

"The Spirit of the Sovereign Lord is on me, because the Lord has anointed me to proclaim good news to the poor. He has sent me to bind up the brokenhearted, to proclaim freedom for the captives and release from darkness for the prisoners, to proclaim the year of the Lord's favor and the day of vengeance of our God, to comfort all who mourn, and provide for those who grieve in Zion—to bestow on them a crown of beauty instead of ashes, the oil of joy instead of mourning, and a garment of praise instead of a spirit of despair. They will be called oaks of righteousness, a planting of the Lord for the display of his splendor."
—Isaiah 61:1–3

Before You return, Jesus, make this Scripture abounding in my life, in Jesus' name!

In Jesus' Name

"That evening after sunset the people brought to Jesus all the sick and demon-possessed. The whole town gathered at the door, and Jesus healed many who had various diseases. He also drove out many demons, but he would not let the demons speak because they knew who he was."
—*Mark 1:32–34*

"He got up, took his mat and walked out in full view of them all. This amazed everyone and they praised God, saying, 'We have never seen anything like this!'"
—*Mark 2:12*

I pray that this devotional causes your faith to soar and your heart to expand. The glory and goodness of God are covering the Earth! God is revealing Himself to those who sit in darkness. They are seeing a glorious light! His power is on display, and His goodness is beyond our ability to comprehend.

On one of my trips to South Asia, we gathered 1,600 people together to hear the gospel in a radically Islamic country. More than 1,000 gave their lives to Jesus, and scores of people testified to the healing power of Jesus! After the service was over, the people brought their sick and hurting to the front to be prayed for.

As I was receiving people and praying for them, a couple brought their 7-year-old son to me. He had not been able to walk, and his tiny legs were atrophied. I looked around for some reinforcement from my team, thinking, "I need the partnership of another's faith for this one." All of my teammates were busy praying for people; it was just Jesus and me. I began to pray and call on the name of Jesus to do what only He could do. And sure enough, those little legs began to walk! Read the story from the church leader who wrote down the testimony:

> "Our house church team invited a Hindu family from a same area, their 7 years son is paralyzed since birth he never walked but team shared about Jesus, his miracle working power still works among all people without discrimination. They came on bus with faith that Jesus will hear their cry and at the end while Sister Julie and team were praying for people, Parkash brings his paralyzed son for prayer. As sister Julie finished the boy told his mother (later when they reach home) that something touched my legs and I felt something very warm went like electricity in my legs. Immediately, 7 years old boy who never walked he start walking and family went home rejoicing what Jesus have done for them. Now Prakash and his family accepted the Lord as their Savior and telling everyone in their district what Jesus have done for them."

This precious Hindu family had worshiped millions of gods, and none of them heard their cries for mercy. But our Jehovah Raffa did, and with healing and salvation, this entire family was anchored in an eternal hope that can never spoil or fade!

Read a few other testimonies from that evening:

Bhatti, a 19-year-old boy, shared that while the team was praying for the sick and needy, he was touched by the power of God and healed from colic pain and stomach issues.

Barkat, 27 years old, testified that while hearing from some teammates, she was touched by the presence of the Holy Spirit and gave her life to Jesus, accepting Him as her personal Savior. She has a desire to serve the Lord as a missionary.

Boota, a 52-year-old Muslim man, had pain in his kidneys and chest for the last 19 years. Sometimes, the pain was so unbearable that he thought it would be better for him to die. He had no money to go to the doctor. But someone told Boota about our gathering in the city called "Jesus is Risen." Even though he is Muslim, he was told he could join and that Jesus would heal him. After the healing prayer, he felt the pain completely disappear from his body and didn't understand what had happened. But after many days, he slept without pain and understood that Jesus had healed him completely.

Saima shared that she had a notable-sized tumor or cyst in her body for more than 17 years and sometimes felt pain. While she was being prayed for, she felt electricity in her body, and in a few seconds, she noticed the tumor had disappeared. She was shocked but realized Jesus healed her pain and tumor!

God is on the move across the globe, bringing scores of people to Himself! They are running to Him in droves, and He is pouring out His love on them, healing their diseases, and setting them free! There is no greater adventure than following Jesus, and it's worth our whole lives!

"'I, the Lord, have called you in righteousness; I will take hold of your hand. I will keep you and will make you to be a covenant for the people and a light for the Gentiles, to open eyes that are blind, to free captives from prison and to release from the dungeon those who sit in darkness. I am the Lord; that is my name! I will not yield my glory to another or my praise to idols.'"
–Isaiah 42:6–8

NUMBERING OUR DAYS

*"'Show me, Lord, my life's end and the number of my days;
let me know how fleeting my life is. You have made my days a
mere handbreadth; the span of my years is as nothing before you.
Everyone is but a breath, even those who seem secure.'"*
—Psalm 39:4–5

"Teach us to number our days, that we may gain a heart of wisdom."
—Psalm 90:12

I have been hit recently with the profundity of how short life is. There are a few whom I love who are battling cancer. Life speeds by, and what once felt like a year of time now only feels like six months. As I keep my eye on the Word and current events, even end-time events seem to be unfolding at a more rapid pace. The European Central Bank's digital euro is being expedited to roll out in the next few years. We are quickening the speed to one world, one currency, and the red carpet to one leader who will take center stage.

This has been the pondering of my heart before the Lord: How am I to live the next few years with this current administration in America that has given me the ability to move in freedom to the nations? What is the

best yes in my life for the next 30 months? With that, I often meditate on
the following Scriptures:

*"The end of all things is near. Therefore be alert and of
sober mind so that you may pray. Above all, love each other
deeply, because love covers over a multitude of sins."*
–1 Peter 4:7–8

*"'So you also must be ready, because the Son of Man will
come at an hour when you do not expect him.'"*
–Matthew 24:44

*"'Be always on the watch, and pray that you may be able to escape all that is
about to happen, and that you may be able to stand before the Son of Man.'"*
–Luke 21:36

In our ever-present sufferings from living in a broken world, we are
compelled to hold on to the hope of Heaven. But what do we do when
we are living in freedom and prosperity and our resources are increasing
in our nation to the point where we don't need to depend on God? How
do we live then? I want to take you back to something I wrote earlier this
year: "We must resist the urge to be lulled into complacency. The Church
must awaken to her mission. We live in turbulent times. The signs point
us toward urgency, not comfort. As followers of Christ, we are called to
carry the gospel to the ends of the Earth, not retreat into personal ease or
self-preservation."

There is a great tension that exists; I would even define it as a
battle for the soul of the Church in America. In these days of peace and
prosperity, what is the pace of advancement for the Church? Do we buy
new comfortable pews, or do we fit the saints with shoes shod with the
gospel of peace?

I have had a sense of urgency in my heart for a few years now, but it is ever-increasing as we have a small window to go and preach the gospel. The borders are open for us to go nearly all over the world. When I am in countries where lostness is so great, I feel the hunger for Jesus, and I see it in the responses of the people I share with. God is moving in power, and His goodness and love are ushering many into the Kingdom. How can I, therefore, devote my life to the purposes of God?

As we are pursuing revival these 40 days, and with the end in mind, I invite you to develop your own personal mission and vision for the next 30 months. I am doing the same so that I have no regrets at the beginning of 2029. Here are a few questions to help you formulate this with the Lord.

1. **What is Holy Spirit highlighting in this season of my life, and what is He inviting me to steward more intentionally?**

This question helps you align your vision with divine timing and purpose, focusing on areas where you feel spiritual prompting, conviction, or opportunity.

2. **What core values, passions, or burdens consistently stir my heart, even when no one is watching?**

This helps clarify the deeper "why" behind your actions and points to your mission—the unique impact you're called to make.

3. **Where do I sense the most fruit, favor, and growth happening, and how can I multiply that?**

This shapes a strategy for the next 30 months based on what is already working, bearing fruit, or showing potential for greater influence.

4. **At the end of these 30 months, what would I want to be true
    of my character, relationships, and legacy?**

This creates a forward-looking, holistic vision—one that encompasses
personal, spiritual, and relational goals, not just accomplishments.

*"'But you will receive power when the Holy Spirit comes on
you; and you will be my witnesses in Jerusalem, and in all
Judea and Samaria, and to the ends of the earth.'"*
—Acts 1:8

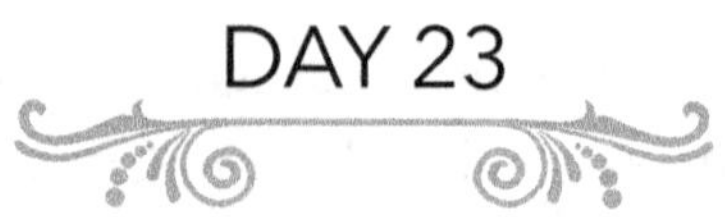

HIS OUTPOURING

*"'This is my blood of the covenant, which is poured
out for many for the forgiveness of sins.'"*
–Matthew 26:28

Every week, we take communion at church. And every week, we read this Scripture. But this week, the words "poured out" gripped me as though I had never read them before. His blood was poured out for us—every last drop. He gave everything for us—absolutely everything!

We are completely forgiven.

We are totally cleansed and have been made the righteousness of Christ.

We have received the holiness and perfection of Christ in completion.

We have been given a new covenant of grace; the law has been fulfilled.

He poured out His blood, and then He poured out His Spirit, His love, and His grace.

""In the last days, God says, I will pour out my Spirit on all people. Your
sons and daughters will prophesy, your young men will see visions, your
old men will dream dreams. Even on my servants, both men and women,
I will pour out my Spirit in those days, and they will prophesy.""
—Acts 2:17–18

"And hope does not put us to shame, because God's love has been poured
out into our hearts through the Holy Spirit, who has been given to us."
—Romans 5:5

"The grace of our Lord was poured out on me abundantly,
along with the faith and love that are in Christ Jesus."
—1 Timothy 1:14

Jesus has poured out, in abundance, the fullness of who He is. He exudes love, grace, and forgiveness; it's His very character. And He wants to pour out the abundance of who He is in what can be received and yet not contained—vessels who are open to receiving the fullness of Christ given to us so that the world can, in turn, receive Him through us. All He is and all He wants to do in abundance are at our disposal. But, are we open to containing the outpouring?

Do we have the faith to receive it and therefore give it? Am I willing, available, and receptive to what God wants to do through my life, which is an open container, without a lid, for His Spirit to flow? Honestly, these are the questions I ponder when a Hindu couple brings me their paralyzed son. These are the questions when 20 prostitutes who are sick and abused are sitting before me, needing the new life of Christ and Christ's wholeness. These are the questions I ask when my girlfriend calls needing deliverance.

His promises to pour it out will be fulfilled because of the New Covenant in His blood. But will His life be manifested more through those who are hungry, desperate, and surrendered? I believe so. Let me explain why. If a believer is skeptical of the works of God and therefore doubts and denies the abundant work of the Spirit due to unbelief, how can one receive what God desires to pour out? We have to take the proverbial lids off our faith in these critical days. He desires to pour out His goodness, blessing, and abundant work of His Spirit. Are we willing to receive it?

> "I ask, what has God promised you, and what can God do to fill a vessel absolutely surrendered to Him? Oh, God wants to bless you in a way beyond what you expect. From the beginning, ear hath not heard, neither hath the eye seen, what God hath prepared for them that wait for Him. God has prepared unheard-of-things, blessings much more wonderful than you can imagine, more mighty than you can conceive. They are divine blessings. Oh, say now: 'I give myself absolutely to God, to do His will, to do only what God wants.' It is God who will enable you to carry out the surrender." –Andrew Murray, "Absolute Surrender" [9]

As He teaches us to number our days and live according to the counsel of His Spirit and His timelines, revival begins in our surrender. Revival is maintained through our surrender. Revival will cover the Earth in the form of God's glory when God's people live in utter surrender to His will, on Earth as it is in Heaven. May Paul's words become the cry of our hearts:

> *"And now, compelled by the Spirit, I am going to Jerusalem, not knowing what will happen to me there. I only know that in every city the Holy Spirit warns me that prison and hardships are facing me.* ***However, I consider my life worth nothing to me; my only aim is to finish the race and complete the task the Lord Jesus has given me—the task of testifying to the good news of God's grace."***
> *–Acts 20:22-24, emphasis added*

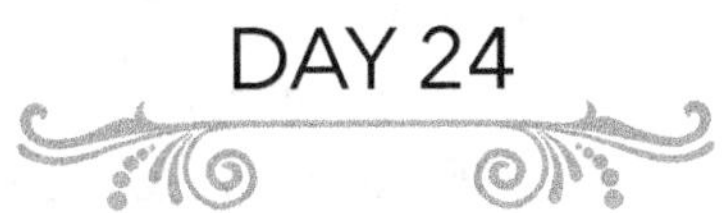

CHANGE COURSE

"For everyone looks out for their own interests, not those of Jesus Christ."
–Philippians 2:21

What a stinging verse that I'm not sure I ever paid that close of attention to. Everyone? I think if I really got honest before the Lord, it means me, too. May it not be so, Jesus.

I have a sound in my spirit that is longing to find words. In summary, it's the essence of two things: 1) it's time for the Church in America to awaken, and 2) we must arise and take hold of these critical days in which we have been assigned. We long for revival but believe someone else will bring it. We are just fine as is. Keep pressing forward as normal, full steam ahead.

One weekend, we toured Titanic: The Exhibition in Dallas, Texas. It felt very prophetic to me as we walked through it. The warnings were so very clear to Captain Smith but altogether ignored. It could have been prevented had warnings been heeded, but pride and arrogance to be the best kept them moving forward at great speed.

Here are the "Final Moments: Ignoring the Warnings" that were summarized at the exhibit:

"On Sunday, April 14, *Titanic* received warnings of icebergs ahead, and smaller chunks of ice known as growlers. Still, Captain Smith was not concerned and maintained full speed. Marconi radio operator Jack Phillips received messages about fields of bergs and pack ice. At 11:00 p.m., the *SS Californian* radioed that it had stopped amid ice. As *Titanic* sailed closer toward danger, Phillips put the warning messages aside to continue sending passenger telegrams about *Titanic's* grand amenities and promising soon to be in New York."

Paul was writing this word to the church in Philippi, mentioning how Timothy was uniquely selfless and genuinely concerned for the well-being of the Philippian church. This was in direct comparison to others who were preoccupied with their own affairs rather than with the mission and mindset of Christ.

I believe this verse could form a framework for us as we wrestle these 40 days with how our lives will be resituated to carry revival and prioritize Christ in all things.

This is a call to Christ-centered abundance. We think that we are limited to the realm of possibility based on the amount of resources we have or lack. Our natural reality somehow becomes the ceiling of what God can do with us and through us. Our minds are limited in understanding. And yet do you not know that what God has dreamed for you goes beyond what you can even imagine. He has so much more for you! It's time to shift perspective from what we see to what God has for you to do and be! Mindsets of lack and limitation are being shattered, in the name of Jesus!

This is a call to Christ-centered priorities. In a world of individualism, Jesus modeled for us a life of love and sacrifice. In fact, if we carry our cross, it will involve sacrifice. Jesus said, *"""Truly I tell you, whatever you did for one of the least of these brothers and sisters of mine, you did for me (Matthew 25:40)."""* I must continually ask myself if my life is wrapped around the priorities of Christ in the Earth or my own priorities. Remember, the only thing we take with us to Heaven is people. It's what Jesus died for in order to take us to Heaven. Our lives should flow in the same measure of priority, or we need to rearrange.

This is a call to Christ-centered sacrifice. To live for Christ means living like Christ, who emptied Himself and gave up everything. *"In your relationships with one another, have the same mindset as Christ Jesus: Who, being in very nature God, did not consider equality with God something to be used to his own advantage; rather, he made himself nothing by taking the very nature of a servant, being made in human likeness. And being found in appearance as a man, he humbled himself by becoming obedient to death—even death on a cross (Philippians 2:5–8)!"*

This is a call to Christ-centered representation. Christ is inviting us to live in a radical, selfless way that reflects the heart of Christ in a very self-absorbed world. As the world becomes more self-focused, it's an opportunity to look and sound more like Jesus.

At His feet, ask Jesus:

- Am I someone whom God entrusts with His heart, His love, His truth, and His mission?
- Does He trust me with abundance?
- Does He find me faithful in the assignments He gives me, whether small or large?
- Are my daily decisions aligned with what Jesus values?
- When I make plans, do I consider how they serve God's purposes?
- Am I living more for comfort or calling?

The Titanic was surging forward in grand and lavish abundance, not heeding the warnings of danger ahead and adjusting course. Church, may we awaken and arise to reprioritize the interests of Christ in the Church and in the Earth, in Jesus' name!

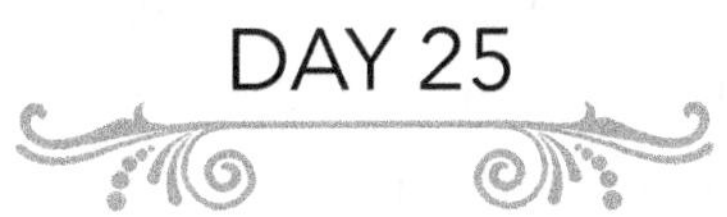

THE LIFE THAT IS REALLY LIFE

"But whatever were gains to me I now consider loss for the sake of
Christ. What is more, I consider everything a loss because of the
surpassing worth of knowing Christ Jesus my Lord, for whose sake I
have lost all things. I consider them garbage, that I may gain Christ
and be found in him, not having a righteousness of my own that
comes from the law, but that which is through faith in Christ—
the righteousness that comes from God on the basis of faith."
–Philippians 3:7–9

In one of the Islamic countries that I travel to, I continue to learn about the lack of value that women hold due to the teaching of the Quran. One of the Quranic teachings is that women are to be viewed as no greater worth than the sole of a man's shoe. They are to be treated as such. Honor killing is permitted in this country if a woman shames her family in any way, and forced conversions are gaining ground for Christians. All they need is a fingerprint on a document, and a woman's rights are gone. That means the freedoms they once held as Christians are eliminated, and they are subject to sharia law, which essentially strips them of any rights.

We know of no such persecution in America. We don't know what it is like to be subjected to a law that strips us of our rights and freedoms.

This is the land of the free and home of the brave. But like I wrote before, are there warnings we are not heeding as we sit in our lavish freedoms and abundance as a Church? We are distracted, comfortable, consumed, and self-indulgent. I include myself in this, and I am wrestling with this in my own heart, to be so honest with you.

Upon my return from the country I spoke of above, I went to a friend's beautiful home. She is quite wealthy, and I celebrate her success. However, when I left, I had a tug in my heart—I want that. Why do I have to be a missionary and not have that? I would be so much happier if I had all that. My heart wrestled between this tension and the Scripture above. It was a battle for my heart.

When Paul in the above Scripture says that he counts these things as a loss, it's not that they were inherently wrong in character; it's that he chose to count them as a loss. He chose to prioritize what was a gain to him, which was Christ and Christ alone.

Here are some beautiful points from David Guzik:

> "It wasn't so much that those things were worthless in themselves, but compared to the greatness of the excellence of the knowledge of Christ Jesus, they really were nothing. Paul here put a *personal relationship with Jesus Christ* at the very center of the Christian's life. He joyfully accepted the loss of all other things for the greatness of this personal relationship. ... This counting loss was not merely an internal spiritual exercise. Paul had indeed suffered the loss of all things that he might gain Christ. ... Because Paul was in Him, he could renounce his own righteousness and live by the righteousness which is from God by faith. The foundation for his spiritual life was in what Jesus had done for him and not in what he had done, was doing, or would do for Jesus in the future."

This is the ground where we long to drive our stakes deep and build our lives—in the fullness of Christ, who is our very life. But oh, how often the riches of this world still pull at the strings of my heart. Will I ever be free—truly free—from the lure of comfort, distraction, and self-indulgence? Can these lesser loves be crucified, once and for all, buried beneath the weight of a greater glory? My soul aches for that kind of freedom—for in that place, we truly live. That is where real life is found—life to the fullest. Our brothers and sisters in Islamic nations are discovering this joy even in the midst of persecution, their abundance found in Christ alone. Yet here in America, our oppression wears a subtler face—unnoticed until the Spirit breaks in and reorders the very core of who we are.

"Prosperity knits a man to the world. He feels that he is finding his place in it, while really it is finding its place in him."
–C. S. Lewis, "The Screwtape Letters"[10]

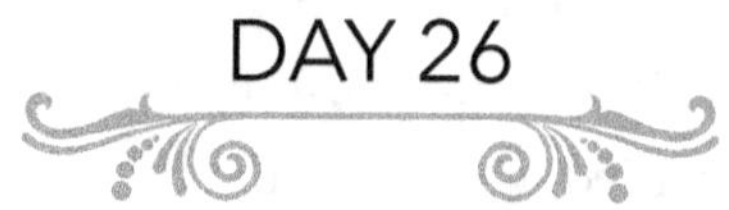

WORTH MY LIFE

*"The Lord's message rang out from you not only in Macedonia
and Achaia—your faith in God has become known everywhere.
Therefore we do not need to say anything about it … ."*
—1 Thessalonians 1:8

*"On the contrary, we speak as those approved by God to be entrusted with
the gospel. We are not trying to please people but God, who tests our hearts."*
—1 Thessalonians 2:4

*"Because we loved you so much, we were delighted to share
with you not only the gospel of God but our lives as well."*
—1 Thessalonians 2:8b

"Indeed, you are our glory and joy."
—1 Thessalonians 2:20

Can't you just hear the deep love Paul had for the people of God in this
letter to the Thessalonians? It rings throughout his writings—all 13
letters—affirming the believers in Christ, for whom he had poured
out his very life. He went from persecuting and imprisoning God's people
to loving them and giving his life for them. The transformation of the

gospel in Paul's own life deposited a deep longing and love for those who were yet to know Christ and those newly established in Jesus.

I found myself, with my small team of five, stuck in a warzone most recently. We were scheduled to share the next day with 20,000 people from 100 different tribal villages. Upon receiving a call from our security department, we had to divert and head back to the main city, canceling the gathering of 20,000 people due to the escalation of the war. I found myself weeping before the Lord that 20,000 were eager to hear about salvation in Christ, and I was running for cover. Here was the reality: I have known the grace and mercy of God for 46 years, but these people have not known it for one hour, let alone a single day. How could I self-preserve when sharing the gospel with these desperate ones was worthy of my life? I wrestled before the Lord, knowing that in that moment, my heart was being marked with a love for a people I had not known. It was a profound encounter with Jesus and one that I will never forget. Even writing this to you brings tears to my eyes.

**I am convinced that the more we become transformed
by love, we cannot help but lay our lives down
for those who do not know our Jesus.**

"Everybody asked, 'Why, what has happened to these Thessalonians? These people have broken their idols: they worship the one God; they trust in Jesus. They are no longer drunken, dishonest, impure, contentious.' Everybody talked of what had taken place among these converted people. Oh, for conversions, plentiful, clear, singular, and manifest; that so the word of God may sound out! Our converts are our best advertisements and arguments." –Charles Spurgeon

I could write pages of testimony of those who live lives that are clear, singular, and manifest for the glory of God; those who have given up wealth and status for lives laid down for the gospel; those who live so counter-cultural in their pursuit of Christ and not the American dream. I can picture a few I know who would dare to die for the gospel. They are my modern-day heroes of the faith, and it's in their going to the world that Heaven will one day be filled with every tribe, tongue, and nation. So, upon the aforementioned Scriptures, I want to challenge you this morning to ask the Lord: Is my life on target with the gospel and Your global purposes for me, written before the foundation of the world?

I bring to you four of Paul's challenges based on our four Scriptures this morning:

Let the Gospel Ring Out From You

Will you pray to live a life so saturated with the gospel that it echoes beyond your community? Refuse to compartmentalize your faith; make your belief in Jesus impossible to ignore. Let your words, your generosity, your hospitality, and your courage make the gospel visible and audible in every sphere of your influence, and in doing so, impact the nations.

Seek the Approval of God Alone

Will you pray to live with the unwavering conviction that God alone is your audience? Reject the temptation to water down truth or live for applause. Embrace your calling as one entrusted with the most precious message on Earth—the gospel of Jesus—and speak it with boldness, humility, and clarity, no matter the cost.

Share Not Just the Gospel But Your Life

Will you pray to break free from transactional or surface-level Christianity? Let your mission to reach others with the gospel also lead you into deep relationships, sacrificial giving, and shared suffering. Open your life, not just your mouth. Be willing to love people all the way to Jesus—through your time, tears, and presence.

Make Disciples Your Joy and Crown

Will you pray to let your deepest joys be found in eternal fruit? Prioritize people over platforms. Pour your life into making disciples who will shine forever. Set your sights on the lost, knowing that the souls you help bring into the Kingdom will be your reward and rejoicing in the presence of Christ.

It is in this that you will find your greatest glory and joy; I promise!

THANK YOU FOR GRACE

*"At Iconium Paul and Barnabas went as usual into the Jewish synagogue. There they **spoke so effectively** that a great number of Jews and Greeks believed. But the Jews who refused to believe stirred up the other Gentiles and poisoned their minds against the brothers. So Paul and Barnabas spent considerable time there, **speaking boldly** for the Lord, who confirmed the message of his grace by **enabling them to perform signs and wonders**. The people of the city were divided; some sided with the Jews, others with the apostles. There was a plot afoot among both Gentiles and Jews, together with their leaders, to mistreat them and stone them. But they found out about it and fled to the Lycaonian cities of Lystra and Derbe and to the surrounding country, where they continued to preach the gospel.*

"In Lystra there sat a man who was lame. He had been that way from birth and had never walked. He listened to Paul as he was speaking. Paul looked directly at him, saw that he had faith to be healed and called out, 'Stand up on your feet!' At that, the man jumped up and began to walk."
—*Acts 14:1–10, emphasis added*

This is such a beautiful illustration of the powerful and scandalous grace of God to and through Paul and Barnabas. Today, we take a moment to pause and celebrate how God's grace touches our lives through salvation, through his sustaining power in trials, and through the privilege of sharing His love with others. Let's trace the cords of grace in this passage.

Once again, we see Paul in the synagogue, preaching to the Jews and Gentiles. If you remember, the last opportunity he had to do this brought great attack. The perseverance of the Spirit of God enabled him to boldly and courageously go back into what surely would be another place of great opposition. Christ in Paul did not want either Jew or Gentile to miss the grace of God. The gift of salvation for those far from Jesus compelled a deep resolve in Paul to persist in the face of persecution. This is profound grace in and through this Christ follower!

The grace of the gospel, through the grace of the Spirit, will take you to places where your human frailty dare not go.

Holding onto your faith in the midst of trials can only come forth from a deep dependence on the Lord. And our very dependence is tied to the wooing love of Holy Spirit by God's grace. It begins with Him! Here we see our two missionaries pressing forward, boldly preaching the gospel and moving in the power of God with signs and wonders. I am sure that the gift of God to heal the lame man touched Paul and Barnabas as much as it touched the lame man. (Paul had surely heard of the miracle at the gate called Beautiful in Acts 3 with Peter.) This kiss from Heaven in the pressure cooker of adversity was none other than the most beautiful gift of grace in that moment. God gives grace to enable His servants to stand firm in opposition so we can endure and continually abide. He often does it with wonder upon wonder.

I can remember a moment on an Extreme Team trip where we were hiking in the Himalayas to reach remote villages to tell the people about Jesus. I had encountered so much suffering this one day that I told the Lord, "I don't think I can do this anymore." We saw people discarded with no human dignity and animals being abused, and my body was weary from the physical demand to endure. In my soul, I was essentially telling the Lord I could not persevere anymore. The next morning, I woke up and could not stop crying. Not being a crier, this was a new experience for me. I knew that Holy Spirit was doing a very deep work in my heart and my will. As I talked with the Lord and wrestled with my weeping and grieving, I came to the conclusion that as long as God gives me the grace and the strength to do these Extreme Teams, I must go. The grace of God pursued me and changed me in my frailty, weakness, and surrender.

Grace brought salvation to you and me, and grace wants to flow out of us with the very same message of love and forgiveness to a world gasping for the oxygen of grace.

Grace was not limited to only the Jews; now the Gentiles were being grafted in. Nor did it belong to just one nation; the ends of the Earth were being included. Grace is available to anyone who responds in faith to Jesus. It is entirely a gift from God. And as we have freely received, we must freely give. Paul and Barnabas lived with the grace of urgency and determination. Will you take hold of this gift of grace that wants to break free from your life like gushing rivers?

> "What is the cost of this kind of discipleship? It is the cross, plain and simple. As a disciple of Jesus Christ, picking up your cross and following Him will involve denying your flesh, and that is costly. The cross comes at a cost to your pride and self-will. God designed it that way. He uses the ugly and difficult things in our lives as instruments of growth toward Christlikeness, which, in turn, clearly display the gospel's transforming power." –Jack Hibbs, "Living in the Daze of Deception"[11]

From this passage of Scripture, we are reminded of the miracles of grace in the following ways:

- God's grace chased you down to bring you salvation and change you forever.
- God's grace is not dependent on your performance or self-righteousness, but rather on His unconditional love and kindness.
- God's grace gives you the ability to stand in trials and face opposition. The same grace that sustained Paul and Barnabas upholds you today.
- God's grace is a gift to be given through your life to people and nations who have never heard His beautiful name.
- God's grace will overwhelm your life, even in your fears and weaknesses, to enable you to be an instrument of His grace so you can boldly share Christ with others.

Christ has qualified you to share in the gift of grace because of all that Jesus gave of Himself so you could have life. He withheld nothing but gave it all for you. Without the cross, resurrection, and ascension, we wouldn't stand a chance! But the righteousness of Christ is now yours forever! That's reason enough to pause and give thanks. Our inheritance as saints and sons and daughters is the abundant result of grace, and Jesus did every work and made every sacrifice so you could stand holy before Him. Since you have so freely received, now freely give it away!

OUR ANTHEM

"Who has believed our message and to whom has the arm of the Lord been revealed? He grew up before him like a tender shoot, and like a root out of dry ground. He had no beauty or majesty to attract us to him, nothing in his appearance that we should desire him. He was despised and rejected by mankind, a man of suffering, and familiar with pain. Like one from whom people hide their faces he was despised, and we held him in low esteem. Surely he took up our pain and bore our suffering, yet we considered him punished by God, stricken by him, and afflicted. But he was pierced for our transgressions, he was crushed for our iniquities; the punishment that brought us peace was on him, and by his wounds we are healed. We all, like sheep, have gone astray, each of us has turned to our own way; and the Lord has laid on him the iniquity of us all."
—Isaiah 53:1–6

As we round third base to home, I celebrate our pursuit of revival together. Oh, that we would be fully awake and alive, knowing the times and seasons, preparing to meet Jesus in the air, and walking in boldness for the sake of the gospel. I pray your heart has been stirred to think beyond the great American dream, building bigger barns, and running toward self-preservation. I pray you have sensed the Spirit stirring the nest of your perceived comfort for the more that He has assigned to you, written before the foundation of the Earth was laid. I pray that your spirit hears the cries of nations beckoning you to come and speak to them the hope and love of Jesus.

Awake and alive, we turn our attention to Isaiah 53, a prophetic passage about our glorious Savior. I have been so drawn to this passage as of late, which is really an evangelistic piece, outlining the simple gospel message. The treasures hidden in Isaiah 53 are worthy of our contemplation, so antithetical to what the Jews were anticipating in their coming Messiah.

In a recent message with Jack Hibbs and Amir Tsarfati, Amir shared how the Jews are turning from materialism, hedonism, and secularism to God. They pray every day for the "return of the Messiah." Jesus came, and they missed Him. During the tribulation, they will not miss Him again. There will be 144,000 from all 12 tribes among the bold proclamation of the gospel to the North, South, East, and West!

May our hearts be transformed by these hidden treasures that we don't want to miss as we pursue revival.

Heaven's glory was wrapped in humility, unnoticed by the world but exalted by God. What if our lives, emptied of self, echoed the same hidden power?

What the world despised, God glorified. Jesus came in humility and quietness as a tender shoot. He had no physical appeal but carried the very presence of God. The world overlooked Him. He was not the spectacle king that the Jews were anticipating. But Jesus did the will of the Father, and His life was subjected and surrendered unto that end. What if our pursuit of followers and publicity was crucified for the mere attention and affection of only One—our Jesus? What if, in our love and surrender to Jesus, life got less distracted, more focused, and made the gates of Hell tremble? What if we became unnoticed and overlooked in the natural but had such a reverberating impact in the spiritual?

Jesus doesn't avoid our pain; He carries it, redeems it, and invites us to meet others in theirs with the healing we've received.

Jesus is familiar with our pain. He entered into our suffering, fully aware of our broken condition. But our Savior and Healer accomplished our healing and wholeness in His afflicted body. Every wound was for you. Every lashing had your name on it. The profound depth of suffering Jesus endured was for you. He is not distant in your afflictions; rather, He enters into them. He is not indifferent to your wounds; He carries them. You are deeply known and deeply loved. It's in your brokenness that the God of the universe bends His ear to hear the cries of your heart. And it's in your brokenness and healing that you enter into the sufferings of others and proclaim to them the faithfulness of your Savior.

The cross compels us not just to worship but to go because what we freely receive in Christ, the nations still lack.

Your innocent Savior suffered to bear your guilt and shame. Your peace was purchased through His pain. I can't live a day without the grace and mercy of God. This is what compels me to the nations. They have lived their whole existence not knowing the peace, presence, hope, love, grace, and mercy of Jesus, while I soak, breathe, and relish in it. Beholding the cross and receiving the holy exchange of our human experience, the suffering of Jesus provokes awe and gratitude, repentance and joy.

Revival begins with the revelation of the cross, our desperation for Jesus, and the decision to live in surrender to the will of the Father. Not my will, but Yours be done. Not my agenda, but Your plans and purposes fulfilled in my life. Revival is 100% about the gospel—our understanding and reception of His finished work, proclaimed boldly through a surrendered life. This is our anthem.

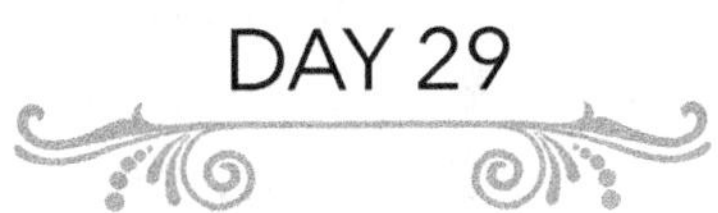

CRUSHED AND COMPELLED

"Yet it was the Lord's will to crush him and cause him to suffer, and though the Lord makes his life an offering for sin, he will see his offspring and prolong his days, and the will of the Lord will prosper in his hand. After he has suffered, he will see the light of life and be satisfied; by his knowledge my righteous servant will justify many, and he will bear their iniquities. Therefore I will give him a portion among the great, and he will divide the spoils with the strong, because he poured out his life unto death, and was numbered with the transgressors. For he bore the sin of many, and made intercession for the transgressors."
–Isaiah 53:10–12

Does this passage not compel you to worship? Oh, that we would fall deeper in love with Jesus. Every word of this prophecy in Isaiah 53 was fulfilled—not one detail was missed. And the fruit of that crushed life continues to be poured out on dry, lost souls so they can find life. But it also continues to be poured out on you that you may be sanctified, healed, and set free.

In fact, the healing you pray to receive is meant to be the gift you are to give to others. You know how to persevere in prayer. You know how to hold on to the Word of God. In fact, you also know a new authority as an overcomer that God intends for you to give away. The healing Jesus afforded to you is now to be given away. Freely give as you have received.

My dear friend Becky battled Lyme disease so severely. It had been debilitating for years. God was drawing Becky's heart to serve the Lord throughout the nations. So in faith, she signed up to go to South Asia with me. The week before we left, she was bedridden in such severe pain. Still confident that God had called her, she packed her bag and headed to the airport. Her faith and the barrier of her body were in direct collision. As the wheels of the plane took off, all of the pain in Becky's body left, and she was entirely healed and set free. Now she takes around eight teams a year to the nations because she knows she was healed so she could tell others about Jesus. That's the heart of this passage I want you to grasp!

Jesus was crushed, wounded, and suffered not for his own gain, but for yours. The full scope of what was done for you and me is hard to comprehend. But we live every moment, every breath, under the weight of this glorious gift of grace, love, and mercy. We take hold of it, and it anchors our souls. But what about those who have never tasted or seen His goodness? Is that our responsibility? My responsibility? Maybe someone else's?

Last night, the Lord spoke to me two words: "spiritual loitering." The definition of loitering is to stand or wait around idly or without apparent purpose. As I ponder this phrase, I fear that the American church is in such a stance. The truth of the matter is, we have Christ in us—all of Him, fully dwelling in us. But "spiritual loitering" still compels us to stand around spiritually, circling round and round with no apparent purpose. I have women often tell me, "I just don't know what my purpose is." Most have spent decades in Bible studies and could teach in seminaries in most countries. But they are directionless; they are close to the Church and love Jesus, but don't know how to live in these end of days. So many have taken hold of their forgiveness and healing and, yet, are standing still.

Church, we can't afford to do this any longer. I beseech you to ask the Lord if you are spiritually loitering in these critical days.

Three treasures I want to share with you:

> *"Yet it was the Lord's will to crush him and cause him to suffer ... (Isaiah 53:10a)."* The word "will" means delight or pleasure. God delighted in what the suffering of Christ accomplished—the salvation of many. God will not waste your crushing. It will produce fruit for those who need the testimony of what Christ has done for you.

> *"... he will see his offspring and prolong his days ... (Isaiah 53:10b)."* You are the offspring of Christ, sent to the world to bring this very resurrection power to the dying and lost.

> *"... my righteous servant will justify many, and he will bear their iniquities ... (Isaiah 53:11b)."* He has made the guilty righteous before God. This is a deep, legal, and spiritual transformation. And He commissions you by His Spirit to be a messenger of reconciliation.

Go in the fully accomplished purposes of Christ. Jesus did, as God designed it from the beginning. And so, we go—not waiting or standing around purposeless—to the lost and dying while we still can!

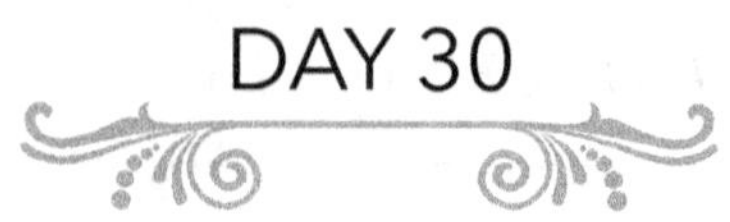

DRESSED, BURNING, WATCHING, WAITING

"Let your waist be girded and your lamps burning; and you yourselves be like men who wait for their master, when he will return from the wedding, that when he comes and knocks they may open to him immediately. Blessed are those servants whom the master, when he comes, will find watching. Assuredly, I say to you that he will gird himself and have them sit down to eat, and will come and serve them. And if he should come in the second watch, or come in the third watch, and find them so, blessed are those servants."'
–Luke 12:35–38, NKJV

Recently, my thoughts have been consumed with a woman we found in a forgotten village deep in a desert in South Asia. She was just skin and bones, greatly abused and oppressed. Her eyes told a story of being forsaken and forgotten. She may have had weeks left of life, as she had given up the will to live. She came into the clinic, having just received Jesus as her Savior, looking for help. I will never forget her.

This devotional has been burning in my spirit as the Lord took me to this passage of Scripture. For those in the Body of Christ crying out, "Maranatha," we don't wait in vain. Jesus told His precious disciples, in the midst of a large crowd, some very intimate words in preparation for the rapture of the Church. The ones closest to Him received secret instruction as to how we are to get ready.

Our loose outer clothing needs to be tied up and ready for action, with the belt of truth around our waist. This was a reference to Exodus 12:11: *"'This is how you are to eat it: with your cloak tucked into your belt, your sandals on your feet and your staff in your hand. Eat it in haste; it is the Lord's Passover.'"* Remember when Elijah outran the chariot because rain was coming (1 Kings 18:46)? We see his outer cloak tied up so he can run and run fast. Are our metaphorical garments prepared to go when the Lord calls us to do something that requires faith and bold action? Or are we sitting around with our gospel shoes in the closet and the belt of truth hanging up for Sunday mornings only? If so, pull them back out. It's time to go!

Our lamps that Jesus was referencing were to be trimmed and filled with oil. You hear His cry to not let your lights go out in His story of the 10 virgins (Matthew 25:1–13). However, what if we ponder the burning to be something that exists in our hearts and in our bones? Does His Word burn in you like Jeremiah spoke of: *"... his word is in my heart like a fire, a fire shut up in my bones. I am weary of holding it in; indeed, I cannot (Jeremiah 20:9)."* Does your love and passion for Jesus burn in you? Is it waning and weary? He longs to reignite it in you because He desires you to walk in the fullness of His abundant life.

The word "watching" means to keep awake, be vigilant, and be watchful. There is nothing more difficult these days than staying undistracted and wide-awake. There are too many things trying to lull us asleep and pull us away from truth. Before Jesus comes for His Bride, there will be a great falling away, called the great apostasy. Many who profess to be followers of Jesus will fall away from the truth. I pray we will remain steadfast and wide-awake!

The last word I want to point your attention to is the word "waiting." In Greek, the word means to await with confidence or patience. The

Christian Standard Bible says, *"Blessed will be those servants the master finds alert when he comes (Luke 12:37)."* This is paralleled with Romans 13:11, which says, *"And do this, understanding the present time: The hour has already come for you to wake up from your slumber, because our salvation is nearer now than when we first believed."*

Remember how our first point of preparation is our attire—dressed and ready? Look at what Jesus will do when He comes; He, too, will get dressed and ready to minister to His Bride. I can't imagine reclining at the table with Jesus as He serves and loves and speaks tenderly to each one of us. We will have made it to our precious finish line and will receive the full reward of our faith—Christ Jesus. It will all make sense then as we gaze upon His beauty, knowing every sacrifice was worth the cost.

> "Those servants who are alert to their master's return will be blessed. So blessed are they, in fact, that the Lord will reverse the roles and serve them by girding up his loins and seating them at the table and serving them." –C. Marvin Pate

Let's look back at the woman sitting in pain and oppression and suffering. She's the face I see when I want to hang up my outer garments. She's the face I see when someone tells me they can't go to take the gospel to the lost. There are more than 3 billion faces that look just like hers. I charge you to get dressed and ready because the Spirit of God is inviting us into something so outlandish and adventurous, your heart couldn't contain it if He showed you. Our watching and waiting isn't reading countless "Rapture Ready" articles. It's knowing the days in which we are living and not measuring our lives against culture but rather against the Words of Jesus. Do His words burn in you? Are they like a fire in your bones you can't contain? Have you fixed your gaze? He's coming, and He's coming soon. How will He find you when He returns? Let's spend our lives pouring out our love for Him, no matter what it costs us!

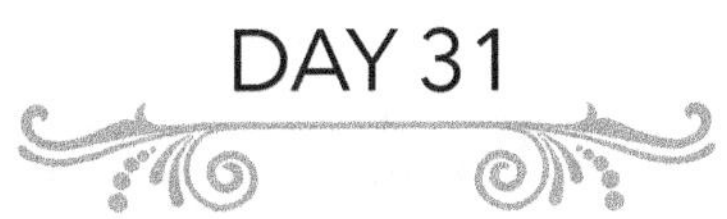

PRAY BIGGER, DREAM WILDER, BELIEVE GREATER

*"Ask me, and I will make the nations your inheritance,
the ends of the earth your possession."'*
–Psalm 2:8

*"The Spirit of the Lord will rest on him—the Spirit of wisdom
and of understanding, the Spirit of counsel and of might,
the Spirit of the knowledge and fear of the Lord ... ."*
–Isaiah 11:2

*"'Enlarge the place of your tent, stretch your tent curtains wide,
do not hold back; lengthen your cords, strengthen your stakes. For
you will spread out to the right and to the left; your descendants
will dispossess nations and settle in their desolate cities."'*
–Isaiah 54:2–3

God's Invitation to Ask Boldly

My desire in this devotional is to inspire and urge you to pray bigger; ask for bold, God-sized dreams; and believe Him for even more than your eyes have yet to see. I want to take you into the intimate pages of my journal because these are the very Scriptures I am clinging to in this season—words that are not just ink on paper but fuel my faith.

> "Lord, today, I ask You for the nations, for Your anointing, and for Your increase. I am asking You to assign me specific nations You have placed on my heart. I pray for doors to open that no man can shut. I pray for increase over my life in calling and anointing for the nations. I pray that You would widen my possession, stretch my capacity, and enlarge the borders of my influence until my life overflows with Kingdom fruit."

What are you asking the Lord for as part of your legacy and inheritance? What will your children carry forth from your life? For those who have not borne children, what will your spiritual children carry forth? Scripture declares:

> *"'Sing, barren woman, you who never bore a child; burst into song, shout for joy … because more are the children of the desolate woman than of her who has a husband,' says the Lord."*
> *–Isaiah 54:1*

When our lives are available to plant the gospel in the next generation, God Himself will multiply our impact. He will raise you up as a spiritual mother—or father—to nations, tribes, and peoples. I see this in the women who faithfully travel with me to the nations, pouring themselves out for others—women like Lizzy, Patti, Alex, and Stacey, who now have countless spiritual sons and daughters scattered across the globe. Heaven will be filled with their offspring—faces and names they may never know this side of eternity. I can picture their children greeting them with joy in Heaven one day.

What is the possession you hold in your heart or hands that God desires to widen?

David began as a shepherd in the quiet fields. His possession was sheep. He didn't ask to be king, but God was preparing him for more by teaching him to shepherd well. What you hold now may seem small, but in God's eyes, it may be the training ground for something that will shake nations. Don't look at your flock or your field and think, "This is it." The Lord is inviting us to lift our eyes and ask—not just for our street or city but for entire nations. Our vision must match His: vast, borderless, and burning with His love for the whole Earth.

The Spirit Empowers the Mission

On the foundation of bold prayers, the Spirit of the Lord will rest on His people with wisdom, counsel, and might. Revival is never sustained by mere human strategy; it is carried by the weight of His presence. He will open your eyes to see what He sees, to feel what He feels, and to partner with Him in bringing His plans to pass. I praise God for the women and men in this hour who are stepping forward without hesitation, determined not to shrink back.

Some of my dearest friends—Rose Ann, Charlotte, Lucy, Sandy, and Joy—are in their 80s. Yet, in the last two years, each one raised her hand and said, "Send me, Lord." They refused to be bound by limitations, excuses, or the voice of fear. They simply obeyed. And in His perfect timing, God is fulfilling through them the assignments He prepared long before they were knit together in their mothers' wombs. Watching them walk this path is nothing short of wonder. I honor them greatly.

The Call to Expand Beyond Our Comfort Zones

Revival always stretches us. It pushes us beyond what feels safe or predictable. It asks us to make room in the very places we've declared too small or too weak. But here's the truth: God is not looking for the strongest or most qualified; He is looking for the surrendered. And when our hearts say, "Yes," He moves with power that defies human logic and opens doors no one else can touch.

> This is our moment.
> Ask boldly.
> Receive fully.
> Expand fearlessly.

Let the Spirit fall. Let the nations be swept into the Kingdom. And may the cry of our hearts echo through eternity:

"Lord, let revival come—and let it begin with us."

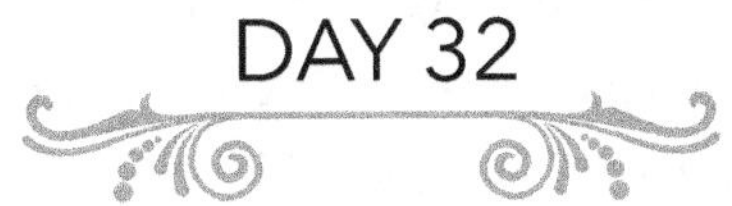

A Single Seed

"'Very truly I tell you, unless a kernel of wheat falls to the ground and
dies, it remains only a single seed. But if it dies, it produces many seeds.'"
—John 12:24

Minutes after the assassination of Charlie Kirk, Holy Spirit brought the above Scripture to mind. It was profound since we had not yet received word of Charlie's death. We saw the response of our nation and other nations—many people returning to the Lord and others going to church for the very first time. We heard the gospel preached over the airwaves like no other time in history. College campuses were responding with large gatherings of college students praying and seeking the Lord. I wondered if the revival we have been praying for and waiting for has come to our shores. Time will tell. But we pray and believe that God is turning the hearts of the fathers to their children and the hearts of children to their fathers (Malachi 4:6).

Do you know that there are not two churches—the persecuted Church and the Church. No, there is just one Church, and half of our Body is enduring persecution all over the world. But as we know in Acts, it's from these fallen seeds, broken open, that many seeds are produced and the Kingdom of God is expanded.

Do you know why America was birthed? Do you know why God set you in this land at this moment of history? Our mandate as a nation has been to preach the gospel to the world. Your calling in life is integrated into that because you bear the name of Jesus and live to bring Him glory. If we have learned anything from the tragedy of Charlie Kirk's death, it's that it is time to find our voice again and not be silent but to courageously and boldly speak for the sake of the gospel. This is something our persecuted brothers and sisters know well.

> "The time for complacency, as if there ever was one, is long past. It is time to engage those warring against biblical Christianity by taking a bold stand. And by a bold stand, I mean living out a biblically based passionate bold faith—resilient, immovable, and incredibly effective in the last days. Doing anything less neutralizes the church, rendering it ineffective in fulfilling its calling to spread the gospel and make disciples of Jesus Christ. It causes our faith to cease being relevant, useful, or capable of being salt and light. In a word, bold!" –Jack Hibbs, "Called to Take a Bold Stand"[12]

Beloved Church, this is our hour! It's not our hour because one of our brothers in Christ was assassinated in America. It's our hour because we have been entrusted with a most precious gift and calling—to make Jesus known all over the Earth, raise up an army of worshippers in the darkest places of the globe, and fulfill our Kingdom mandate. This will require broken, humbled, surrendered vessels who count their lives as nothing. It will require not measuring cost against reward because we know our reward awaits us in Heaven. It will require a level of surrender and faith that the Spirit of God will give you if you will simply ask Him.

I had a woman email me last week, "I have never gone out to talk to people about Christ, and I would like to stop loitering. I am that lady that has spent years in Bible study and around other Christians, and I need to bring the lost to Jesus, but I don't know how." That was the most precious email I have received in a long time! The hunger, humility, and honesty made this such a beautiful response. I want to train you! I want to come and share the simplicity of how to engage others in spiritual conversations. We are looking for opportunities where one woman will pull a group together of hungry, eager women (and men), and we will train and encourage and help you get your feet under you. Simply reach out to me, and we will connect.

Let me close with a prayer for you:

> Father, in the name of Jesus, I pray for my brothers and sisters who are finding their voice in this hour. I pray that You would fill them with courage, boldness, resilience, and vision. I pray for their calling to become crystal clear as they stand at the precipice of something new. I ask You, Lord, to anoint their spiritual eyes to see what You have for them moving forward. Give them the courage to engage the lost in spiritual conversations. Give them a supernatural love for the lost. I pray, Jesus, that You would deposit eternity in their hearts. Fill us with surrender, humility, and faith, in the name of Jesus!

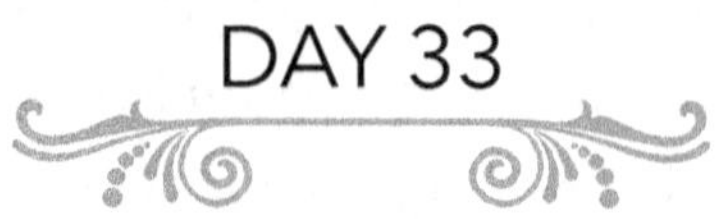

REDEFINED

"I thank Christ Jesus our Lord, who has given me strength, that he considered me trustworthy, appointing me to his service. Even though I was once a blasphemer and a persecutor and a violent man, I was shown mercy because I acted in ignorance and unbelief. The grace of our Lord was poured out on me abundantly, along with the faith and love that are in Christ Jesus.

"Here is a trustworthy saying that deserves full acceptance: Christ Jesus came into the world to save sinners—of whom I am the worst. But for that very reason I was shown mercy so that in me, the worst of sinners, Christ Jesus might display his immense patience as an example for those who would believe in him and receive eternal life."
–1 Timothy 1:12–16

This is our testimony for those of us who know Jesus as our Lord and Savior: while we were still sinners, Christ died for us so that we could display and proclaim His all-surpassing mercy and grace to a people who know nothing of it! Our salvation was meant to be proclaimed, not hidden under a rock.

Paul was so aware of his past and yet not bound by it. He could remember and yet was redefined by the mercy and grace of God. We have the opportunity to help people find mercy and grace and forever have a changed story.

"After Paul was saved, he became the foremost saint. The Lord did not allot him a second-class place in the church. He had been the leading sinner, but his Lord did not, therefore, say, 'I save you, but I shall always remember your wickedness to your disadvantage.' Not so: he counted him faithful, putting him into the ministry and into the apostleship, so that he was not a whit behind the very chief of apostles. Brother, there is no reason why, if you have gone very far in sin, you should not go equally far in usefulness." –Charles Spurgeon

Paul was not disqualified. He was qualified by the blood of Jesus. The victory of Christ was Paul's solid ground—the blood-bought territory his life now stood upon.

Paul writes his statement of calling and identity in 2 Timothy: *"Paul, an apostle of Jesus Christ by the will of God, according to the **promise of life** that is in Christ Jesus … (2 Timothy 1:1, ESV, emphasis added)."* This promise of life, that which can never be taken from us, was greater than Paul's circumstances as he wrote 2 Timothy from a prison in Rome. It went beyond all past memories of a wretched past. It anchored Paul in the reality of the full and eternal life of Christ, despite the past and present. The victory of Jesus was for Paul's past, his present, and his glorious future!

I am reading a beautiful book by Dane Ortlund titled "Deeper." Wrap your heart around these words:

"One reason our spiritual growth grinds down is that we gradually lose a heart sense of the profound length to which Jesus went to save us. *Save* us. When we were running full speed the other direction, he chased us down, subdued our rebellion, and opened our eyes to see our need of him and his all-sufficiency to meet that need. We were not drowning, in need of being thrown a life preserver; we were stone-dead at the bottom of the ocean. He pulled us up, breathed new life into us, and set us on our feet—and every breath we now draw is owing to his full and utter deliverance of us in all our helplessness and death."[13]

You see, as we pursue revival and explore the depths of where God desires to take us, it's passages like these that we remember. We remember where we came from and the length to which Jesus has saved and restored us. And from this place we go!

Paul's life reminds us that the very places of our greatest failure can become the platforms of God's greatest glory. Our past does not disqualify us—it magnifies the mercy of Christ. What once marked us with shame now becomes a testimony of His saving power. In revival, God takes ordinary, broken people and sets them ablaze with His Spirit so the world may see His immeasurable grace on display.

As we seek revival, let us never lose sight of the miracle of our own salvation. We were once dead, but Christ made us alive. We were once lost, but now we are found. And just as Paul was entrusted with the gospel, so, too, are we appointed to carry this message of mercy, grace, and life into a world desperate for hope. Revival begins when we remember what Christ has done for us, and it continues as we boldly proclaim that same mercy to others. From this place of gratitude and awe, we go—anchored in His life, qualified by His blood, and empowered by His Spirit.

DAY 34

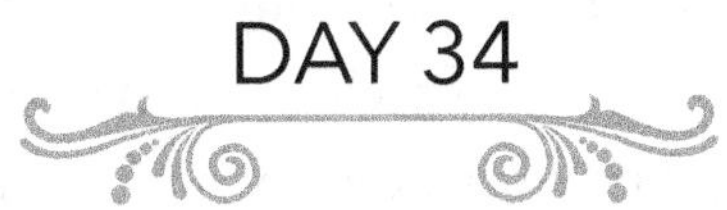

EXPLORE THE DEPTHS

"'Here I am! I stand at the door and knock. If anyone hears my voice and opens the door, I will come in and eat with that person, and they with me.'"
—Revelation 3:20

Jesus is standing at the door of this day, knocking. He's prepared a table before you in the presence of your enemies, many of whom are listed below. He's come to dine with you and speak intimately with you. He's prepared a feast for you and pulled up a chair. There's no need to try and look a certain way or fix yourself before you come. He just wants you—the worn out, overworked, disillusioned, tired, discontented, and curious **you**. There's nothing more healing than His presence. Yesterday, we remembered where we came from. Today, we are doing the same, but we are taking a step forward. He's knocking, so we walk to the door and open it. On the other side of what you are facing is your Savior, with nail-pierced hands, reaching to take yours. He wants to sit and restore you, deep unto deep.

- He stands at the door of pain and asks if you will let Him come and restore your soul.
- He stands at the door of suffering and asks you to place the injustice in His hands.
- He stands at the door of regret and asks you to forgive yourself and receive His forgiveness.

- He stands at the door of disillusionment and asks you to fix your eyes and heart on Him.
- He stands at the door of spiritual hunger and brings you a feast today.
- He stands at the door of feeling trapped by your situation and asks if you will just trust Him today to carry you. His arms are strong enough.
- He stands at the door of financial ruin and asks you to buy from Him treasures that will last for eternity (Revelation 3:18).
- He stands at the door of cancer and asks you to dine with your Jehovah Rapha.
- He stands at the door of loneliness and asks if you will let Him be your constant companion and closest friend.
- He stands at the door of fear and asks if you will exchange your anxiety for His perfect peace.
- He stands at the door of broken relationships and asks if you will allow Him to heal, reconcile, and make new.
- He stands at the door of exhaustion and asks if you will rest in Him, for His yoke is easy and His burden is light.
- He stands at the door of unanswered prayers and asks if you will trust His timing and sovereignty.
- He stands at the door of shame and asks you to step into the freedom of His grace.
- He stands at the door of loss and grief and asks if you will let Him be your comfort and your hope.
- He stands at the door of doubt and invites you to bring your questions, for He is the truth who never changes.
- He stands at the door of uncertainty about the future and asks if you will walk by faith, hand in hand with Him.
- He stands at the door of pride and asks you to humble yourself, that He may lift you up in due time.
- He stands at the door of past wounds and asks if you will let Him rewrite your story with His healing love.

- He stands at the door of complacency and asks if you will be stirred again with holy fire and passion for His name.
- He stands at the door of your heart and asks if you will open wide—for He longs to come in and dwell with you.

I close with this beautiful segment from "Deeper" by Dane Ortlund:

"You don't have to go through security to get to Jesus. You don't have to get in line or take a ticket. No waving for his attention. No raising your voice to make sure he hears you.

"In your smallness, he notices you. In your sinfulness, he draws near to you. In your anguish, he is in solidarity with you.

"What we see is not only that Jesus is gentle toward you but that he is positively drawn toward you when you are most sure he doesn't want to be. It's not only that he is not repelled by your fallenness—he finds your need an emptiness and sorrow irresistible. He is not slow to meet you in your need. It's the difference between a teenager's alarm going off on a Monday morning, forcing him to drag himself out of bed, and that same teen springing out of bed on Christmas morning. Just look at the Savior in Matthew, Mark, Luke, and John. With whom does he hang out? What draws forth his tears? What gets him out of bed in the morning? With whom does he eat lunch? The sidelined, the hollowed out, those long out of hope, those who have sent their lives into meltdown." [13]

The Holy Spirit placed these words on my heart:

I stand at your door. Will you open it to Me?

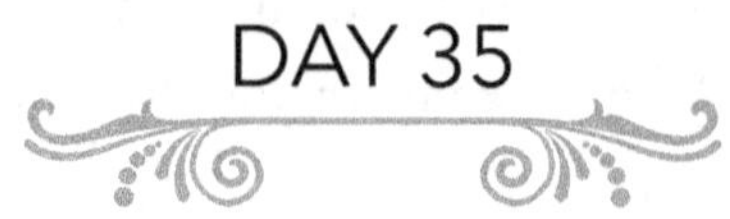

RABBI AND LORD

"When he had finished washing their feet, he put on his clothes and returned to his place. 'Do you understand what I have done for you?' he asked them. 'You call me "Teacher" and "Lord," and rightly so, for that is what I am.'"
—John 13:12–13

The words in my spirit that I want to scribe on paper come from a place of deep tenderness today. I pray I adequately express the invitation sitting on the shores of my own life that I believe Jesus has for us. There's been a lot of injustice and pain that we are all wrestling with in this season. No doubt, we are wrecked and raw. I want to start with a quote that will launch this devotional.

> "Love, for the God of the Bible, is not one activity among others. Love defines who he is most deeply. Ultimate reality is not cold, blank, endless space. Ultimate reality is an eternal fountain of endless, unquenchable love. A love so great and so free that it could not be contained within the uproarious joy of Father, Son, and Spirit but spilled out to create and embrace finite and fallen humans into it. Divine love is inherently spreading, engulfing, embracing, overflowing. If you are a Christian, *God made you so that he could love you.* His embrace of you is the point of your

life. I know you don't feel it. Even that is taken care of. He wants you to know a love that is yours even when you feel undeserving or numb." –Dane Ortlund, "Deeper"[13]

Recently, someone posed the question, "Do we approach the Lord as teacher or as Lord?" In situations and in life in general, are we coming close to our Savior as an instructional rabbi from whom we constantly learn lessons? Or are we coming to Him as Lord—the One we have surrendered the lordship of our lives to, the One who deeply loves and cares for me and you?

Although Jesus affirms both of their approaches in this passage, I want you to look at another scene in Scripture to give this some contrast.

It was the night Jesus was having His last supper with the disciples. He had washed their feet, broken bread, and shared a moment with them in preparation for His departure.

"When evening came, Jesus was reclining at the table with the Twelve. And while they were eating, he said, 'Truly I tell you, one of you will betray me.'

*"They were very sad and began to say to him one after the other, 'Surely you don't mean me, **Lord?**'*

"Jesus replied, 'The one who has dipped his hand into the bowl with me will betray me. The Son of Man will go just as it is written about him. But woe to that man who betrays the Son of Man! It would be better for him if he had not been born.'

*"Then Judas, the one who would betray him, said, 'Surely you don't mean me, **Rabbi?**'*

"Jesus answered, 'You have said so.'"
—Matthew 26:20–25, emphasis added

The disciples were quick to identify the lordship of Jesus, while Judas, who knew nothing intimately of His lordship, simply called Him a teacher. The tenderness of this season begs me to ask the question: What name do you call Him? When a situation pierces your heart, who is He to you? When you are disillusioned, what do you need Him to be? There is no right or wrong answer. But the name by which we call Him can be indicative of how close we feel and really long to be.

Recently, I walked through a season that left me both frustrated and wounded. In the middle of it, someone gently remarked, "Maybe God wants to teach you something." It wasn't a wrong thought, yet deep inside I wondered: What if His desire is not only to instruct me but to hold me? What if He simply longs for me to collapse into His arms and discover that He is the strength of my heart and my portion forever? Perhaps He yearns to be my Comforter and Counselor, my Savior and Restorer—the very Lord of my heart.

Beloved, I want to encourage you, run to Him as Lord. He is far more than just a good teacher. In the midnight hours of our pain, His desire is not merely to inform us but to form us. He listens for the cry of our surrendered hearts calling Him Lord in the midst of shaping, refining, and even suffering. Sometimes, we must allow the names of God to travel the six-inch journey from head to heart—where He ceases to be theory and becomes our living reality.

So I ask you: Will you invite Him to be Lord not only over your joys but also over your despair? Will you shift your gaze from what you can learn to who it is that holds you fast and loves you intimately? Often, what we need most is not a teaching moment but the transformation of His presence. Wisdom, knowledge, and understanding are beautiful gifts, but who He is surpasses what He can teach. In revival, what the world needs is not mere doctrine but the revelation of Jesus as King, Savior, and Rescuer. Take people to your Lord, and trust Him to reveal Himself as Teacher in His perfect timing.

Remember this: He came first to love us before He ever came to teach us.

> *"'Now that I, your Lord and Teacher, have washed your feet,*
> *you also should wash one another's feet.'"*
> *—John 13:14*

Your Lord has not only washed your feet; He has cleansed your whole being—body, soul, and spirit. Carry this reality into a broken world steeped in darkness and pain. As you stoop low to wash the feet of the desperate, revival will burst forth.

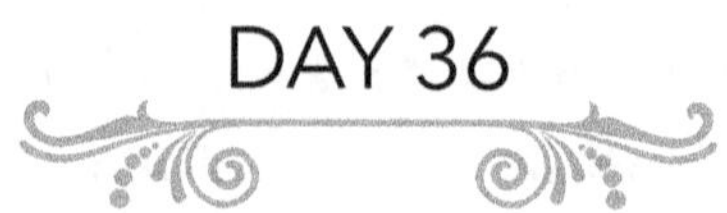

SANCTIFICATION: STORED UP TREASURES

"'A good man brings good things out of the good stored up in him, and an evil man brings evil things out of the evil stored up in him.'"
—Matthew 12:35

"I pray that out of his glorious riches he may strengthen you with power through his Spirit in your inner being, so that Christ may dwell in your hearts through faith. And I pray that you, being rooted and established in love, may have power, together with all the Lord's holy people, to grasp how wide and long and high and deep is the love of Christ, and to know this love that surpasses knowledge— that you may be filled to the measure of all the fullness of God.

"Now to him who is able to do immeasurably more than all we ask or imagine, according to his power that is at work within us, to him be glory in the church and in Christ Jesus throughout all generations, for ever and ever! Amen."
—Ephesians 3:16–21

Recently, I did an intensive security training for the high-risk areas where I do ministry. In one of the simulations, they put black hoods over our heads and zip-tied our hands. We had to be on our knees with our hands outstretched. The goal was to create an anchor in our memory so that if this happens, we know how to breathe and recall Scripture. Each person had their own spiritual experience during this activity. It was very meaningful, even as I reflected on our brothers and sisters who are currently enduring such persecution. That reality took my breath away more than being hooded.

There will be times in our lives when we must draw on what has been stored up inside of us. We dig deep to bring forth the Word that was planted in good soil. I remember leading my daughter, AnnMarie, and four of her girlfriends when she was in middle school. The one thing Holy Spirit had me continually teach them was to store up God's Word in their hearts. Perhaps there was going to come a day when the Bible would not be permitted, and they would need to pull Scripture from the treasure trove of their memory. So it was with me in that hostage exercise.

This brings me to the beautiful work of sanctification God longs to do inside of His people. It's an inward work bearing an outward fruit. I want to make the keen observation that if we try and make the beautiful work of sanctification an outward work by layering our lives with rule upon rule, we misplace the work of the Spirit for behavior and lawful obedience. Look at this quote from my favorite book right now, "Deeper" by Dane Ortlund.

> "Our growth in godliness, in other words, works in an inverse way to justification, both in how it works and in how it gets ruined. In our justification the verdict of legal acquittal must come wholly from heaven, landing on us as something earned by someone outside us, in no way helped out by our contribution. But that has to do with our *standing*. That is the objective result of the gospel.

Sanctification, however, is change with regard to our *walk,*
our personal holiness, the subjective result of the gospel.
This must happen internally."[13]

In essence, what is stored up in us, activated by the deep work of the Holy Spirit, will result in the outward expression of fruitfulness, radical obedience, courageous boldness, and unwavering belief!

Do you believe He can do exceedingly, abundantly more in your life than you have yet to see? The degree to which we desire and anticipate seeing God move has a direct correlation with what we have stored up in our hearts and lives. Someone who lives from an experience of seeing the abundance of God displayed on the Earth will pray and believe for more than someone who has not. Someone who lives in the Word will have a deeper application than those who read God's word at Christmas and Easter.

It all goes back to the words of His Word that we have stored up. These not only become the treasures that we hand to others but also the treasure map we hand to those searching and longing.

So here is the invitation: Sanctification is not about striving harder or layering on rules; it is about storing up the riches of Christ in the depths of who we are, allowing His Spirit to transform us from the inside out. When the trials come, when the hood is pulled over our heads, when the darkness presses in, what rises to the surface will not be panic but peace, not fear but faith, not emptiness but patient endurance.

This is the mystery and the beauty of the gospel: What He plants in us by His Spirit grows into something greater than we could ever manufacture on our own. And from that hidden reservoir flows courage to stand, love that does not quit, and joy that no persecution can steal.

Beloved, what are you storing up today? Because one day, you will reach into the storehouse of your heart, and what you have hidden there will shape your response, your endurance, and your testimony. May it be the Word of God, the love of Christ, and the power of His Spirit that you find.

He is able—able to keep you, able to fill you, able to do immeasurably more than all you ask or imagine. Let Him write His treasure into you so that when the world sees you, what spills out is nothing less than Jesus.

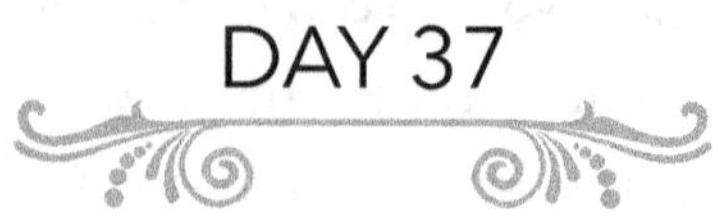

FOUNDATIONS OF REVIVAL

"When I shut up the heavens so that there is no rain, or command locusts to devour the land or send a plague among my people, if my people, who are called by my name, will humble themselves and pray and seek my face and turn from their wicked ways, then I will hear from heaven, and I will forgive their sin and will heal their land. Now my eyes will be open and my ears attentive to the prayers offered in this place."
–2 Chronicles 7:13–15

We have traversed the glorious facets of revival, anchored in the heart of God, carried forth by surrendered vessels. Revival is something I have been praying for since 2007. The cries of my heart were specifically for the awakening of God's people to His purposes in the Earth and then for the lost to be saved. Thank you to those who have traversed this 40-day pursuit of revival alongside me. Thank you for praying desperate prayers with me. Thank you for giving Jesus your yes to what He wants to do in and through your laid down life.

The Scripture above is a thematic Scripture for revival. We, God's people, who bear His name and reflect His glory, walk in the identity as sons and daughters. This is our most secure identity and identification. It's immovable and unshakeable. And it's from this position of belonging, adoption, and redemption we come to Him. In humility, we come to

Him. That means we see ourselves rightly, covered by the blood of Jesus, acknowledging our complete dependence on Him and Him alone.

In repentance, these four things exude from our inner life of surrendering to Jesus: humility, prayer, seeking, and turning. It's not four separate paths to repentance, but the wholeness of what it looks like to fully come, boldly to His throne of grace. This is not a transaction; it's a response of worship as Jesus bids us to come and die. What He has in this great exchange is nothing short of abundant, good, whole, and right. I believe this whole invitation actually begins with the desire of God to heal and forgive. And He shows us how to receive what He longs to pour out on us! It always starts and ends with Him, and if He is the manifest greatness of everything good and marvelous, you better believe He wants to reveal that to hungry, humble ones!

I am learning to live in this space of humility, prayer, seeking, and turning. A common prayer for me has been, "Circumcise my heart, and crucify my flesh." There's a lot of me that needs to learn to die so I can truly live and walk in the abundance of who God is.

Recently, I had the joy and privilege to pray for a woman who developed spinal meningitis more than a year ago. Having a thriving corporate real estate business and a full life, all of a sudden, she found herself one day in the ICU with complete blindness. My friend and I prayed with unwavering faith for God to restore her eyesight. I had such a sense of expectation and hope deep in my spirit. But I also had a sense that when God does bring her eyesight, she will look back on this year as one of the greatest gifts of her life. And she will say, "I wouldn't have given up one day of blindness for the intimacy I have received with Jesus through this season." Sometimes our humility and surrender before the Lord unwraps the gift of a season we could never write for our lives. Pray that Melanie's eyesight will be restored, in Jesus' name. And pray that God downloads into her heart what He has for her coming out of this. I believe His plans for her are profound.

Church, let's continue to root ourselves in our Beloved. Let's find our truest living—our truest purpose—in being united in Christ, cleansed by

His blood, and walking in the "It is finished." Let's throw off everything that is distracting in this season for a life that is surrendered and abandoned to Jesus alone. Let's not make excuses for comfort and complacency; we have done that long enough. The world is looking for sons and daughters who say, *"For to me to live is Christ … (Philippians 1:21),"* who are unashamed of the gospel and proclaim the name of Jesus. Let's get expectant of the full storehouses of Heaven opening before us as we seek the Lord and release His Kingdom in the Earth. Repentance is a gift, not a penance. Turning is an invitation, not a walk of shame. Surrender in humility is our only way forward. If you are willing to die for Jesus, will you be willing to live for Him?

> *"Come, let us return to the Lord. He has torn us to pieces but he will heal us; he has injured us but he will bind up our wounds. After two days he will revive us; on the third day he will restore us, that we may live in his presence. Let us acknowledge the Lord; let us press on to acknowledge him. As surely as the sun rises, he will appear; he will come to us like the winter rains, like the spring rains that water the earth."*
> *—Hosea 6:1–3*

DAY 38

REVIVAL IN THE NATIONS

"Multitudes, multitudes in the valley of decision! For the day of the Lord is near in the valley of decision. The sun and moon will be darkened, and the stars no longer shine. The Lord will roar from Zion and thunder from Jerusalem; the earth and the heavens will tremble. But the Lord will be a refuge for his people, a stronghold for the people of Israel."
—Joel 3:14–16

I recently returned from a country in South Asia that is surprisingly so very hungry for the gospel. I'm finding that where spiritual hunger and seeking exist, God is showing up. He is faithfully revealing Himself to those who are searching for truth and rescue. I want to share a few powerful testimonies to strengthen your faith and give you vision for what God is doing among the nations.

One of my teammates, Alexandria, sat in one of the mud huts. Her chair was partially seated in the toilet area, as the family had a very modest and small abode. She was trying not to focus on the flies and the smell as she presented the clear and simple gospel. This family of five desired to profess faith in Jesus and needed Him to heal their bodies. After my teammate laid hands on each one, they testified to feeling completely healed; all pain was gone! So they left to go and tell their neighbors about the encounter they had with Jesus. Those neighbors came to be prayed for, and Jesus healed them as well. News began spreading like wildfire! Muslims, Hindus, and Christians began coming from the adjacent market to be prayed for. They came in pain and left in freedom! My teammate said that they easily prayed for 100 people, and it would have been many more had they not had to leave.

I wonder at times if this is what Scripture likens to standing under an open Heaven. God just pours out His mercy and grace and power on desperate people. It falls like rain on parched ground. The very power of Jesus touches bodies and woos hearts to a Savior they have never longed for.

> *"I revealed myself to those who did not ask for me; I was found by those who did not seek me. To a nation that did not call on my name, I said, "Here I am, here I am.""*
> *—Isaiah 65:1*

Another one of my teammates, Patti, shared this testimony:

"I shared the gospel with a man and his wife, and they both accepted Jesus as their Lord and Savior. Then I asked if there was anything they would like prayer for, and the husband said he wanted prayer for his knees, that he could only take a few steps. So we prayed God would heal his knees and strengthen his legs. He then tentatively walked a few steps without his cane and then turned around and walked back to his bed. I was encouraged but could tell he was nervous and just asked God to continue the good work He had begun. That afternoon, I saw that same man at the church! I was shocked and delighted to see that he had been able to get there. He had his cane with him, but he evidently was able to walk to the church! My translator and I rejoiced at what the Lord had done!"

I share these testimonies with you to spur on your faith and make your heart eager to taste and see what God is doing in the nations to draw the hungry to Himself. There is no greater privilege than spending our lives on filling Heaven with worshippers from every tribe, tongue, and nation. I invite you to go with us. If you have yet to see these things with your own eyes or have yet to answer the prayer of Jesus to be a laborer in the harvest, I implore you to ask Jesus to send you. Ask Him to make a way for you to go.

Revival always begins with hunger—holy hunger that stirs the heart to move, to go, to pour out, to pray until Heaven touches Earth. The same God who is revealing Himself in South Asia is longing to move in power through us. The nations are trembling in the valley of decision, and the roar of the Lord is being heard again—calling His people to rise, to carry His glory, and to release His compassion to the ends of the Earth. This is not the hour to sit back in comfort; it is the hour to burn with purpose. Let the stories of healing and salvation ignite a cry within you: "Here am I, Lord, send me!" May we be the ones who go where the hunger is great, who stand in the gap, who live to see revival sweep across the nations, and who refuse to rest until the Earth is filled with the knowledge of the glory of the Lord as the waters cover the sea (Habakkuk 2:14).

Let this closing psalm be your heart's cry:

"May God be gracious to us and bless us and make his face shine on us—so that your ways may be known on earth, your salvation among all nations.

"May the peoples praise you, God; may all the peoples praise you. May the nations be glad and sing for joy, for you rule the peoples with equity and guide the nations of the earth. May the peoples praise you, God; may all the peoples praise you.

"The land yields its harvest; God, our God, blesses us. May God bless us still, so that all the ends of the earth will fear him."
—Psalm 67

DAY 39

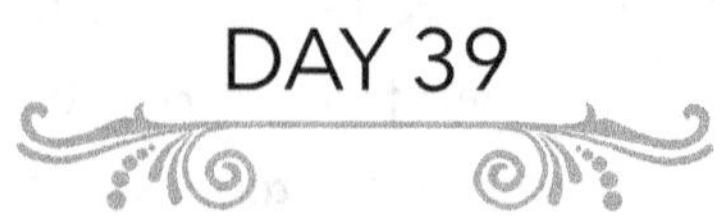

LET THE NATIONS REJOICE

"Look at the nations and watch—and be utterly amazed.
For I am going to do something in your days that you
would not believe, even if you were told.'"
—Habakkuk 1:5

One of the passions of my heart is the fact that, as God has placed eternity in our hearts, we long for the day of Christ's return. Our hearts are fixed on Heaven, and our eyes gaze at the horizon for our coming Bridegroom. There's a two-part endgame to revival: a renewed passion for Jesus that transforms how we view life on Earth, storing up treasures in Heaven; and worshippers filling Heaven for all of eternity from every tribe, tongue, and nation. I often recall the words of one of my translators, "The only thing we take with us to Heaven is people." It's the heartbeat of revival. We begin to walk out what Jesus gave His life for—the redemption of mankind.

It is of late that I can confidently report to you that the nations are hungry for Jesus. I remember my first trip to South Asia in 2017, and only one woman wanted to receive Jesus as her Savior. Now, we travel there, and well over half (if not more) desire to profess faith in Christ. Something has shifted! Hinduism, Islam, Buddhism, and tribal religions aren't delivering what they have promised. But Jesus does every time, and it's glorious to behold. The dreams and visions of the "man in white" all over the Muslim world are drawing scores of people to Jesus in profound numbers.

I recently returned from an Islamic country in South Asia. We shared the gospel and trained indigenous church leaders in how to share the gospel and start gospel movements in their regions. We gather people from 120 tribal villages to hear the gospel of salvation and receive prayer for healing and deliverance. It is glorious to report that we shared with more than 15,000 people and saw upwards of 13,000 profess faith in Jesus! This particular country is on the verge of revival as so many are coming to Christ in this season. One of the pastors we work with knows he has a small window of opportunity before the change of government, so we are seizing the day with boldness and courage.

Before the return of Jesus, we will see the love of many grow cold. We will see wars and earthquakes and tensions in the Earth, pioneered by Hell itself (Matthew 24:6–8, Luke 21:10–11, Revelation 12:12). But we will also see the Bride find her voice and live with a heart cry for the coming of Jesus (Revelation 19:7). The nations will be marked with a move of God, where the Kingdom of God pushes back darkness (Isaiah 60:1–3), and nations will long for Jesus for the first time (Haggai 2:7, Isaiah 2:2–3). The profound aspect of this reality is that Jesus is inviting us to partner with Him to release His presence and power in the Earth and to put Him on display! It's an invitation I urge you to consider!

> "Why has God called you to places like Brazil and Israel, Indonesia and Zimbabwe, and Mexico? Because all over the world people in their poverty and suffering, in their emptiness and sin, are crying out, 'We would see Jesus.' We want to know the Prince of Peace. We want a Savior that can atone for our sins. We want our life of darkness to be illuminated by the Light of the world. But the only chance of their meeting Jesus is for you to go in obedience to God's call—for you to be a mediator like Phillip and introduce

them to the Savior. You see, there is dwelling within you the person of Jesus Christ waiting to be revealed to a lost world. He goes with you and empowers you." –Jerry Rankin, "A Challenge to Great Commission Obedience"[14]

So what does this mean for you today? If you still have breath in your lungs and a cry in your heart that God would use you to fill Heaven and transform Earth, I want to encourage you to pray three powerful words: "God, send me." You have the profound opportunity to be a part of Habakkuk 1:5—to put the glory of God on display in the nations before the return of Christ! There is no greater invitation in all of life than to partner with Father, Son, and Holy Spirit to help fulfill the mission of God beginning in Genesis and ending in Revelation. Could this be the year you see this for the first time with your very own eyes? I want you to seriously consider taking Jesus up on His offer to see the Great Commission brought forth through your very life, your beautiful feet, and a mustard seed of faith.

This is not the hour for passive faith or quiet belief. This is the hour for bold surrender, for burning hearts and willing hands! Heaven is searching for those who will say, "Yes, Lord. Here I am; send me." The same Spirit that raised Christ from the dead is calling you to carry resurrection life into a world gasping for breath. Don't shrink back. Don't wait for another moment, another confirmation, another convenient time. The King is coming, and He is raising up His Bride to shine with unstoppable love and unshakable power.

Step into the story God is writing across the Earth. Let your life be the answer to the groan of creation and the cry of the nations. Say, "Yes," to the fire of His calling. Say, "Yes," to the Great Commission that burns in His heart. Say, "Yes," to being part of the generation that prepares the way of the Lord. The time is now. The harvest is ripe. The invitation is yours. Will you go?

"There is no greater adventure in life than following Jesus to the ends of the Earth." –Evaleen Harris (my mom)

 JULIE KING

DAY 40

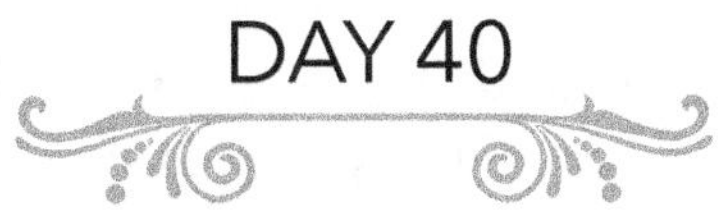

Triumph and Victory

*"But thanks be to God! He gives us the victory through our Lord
Jesus Christ! Therefore my dear brothers and sisters, stand firm. Let
nothing move you. Always give yourselves fully to the work of the Lord,
because you know that your labor in the Lord is not in vain."*
–1 Corinthians 15:57-58, emphasis added

It is truly time to celebrate. The whole world is being confronted
with the reality of sin and brokenness. Our cries for the coming
of Jesus are growing louder! Today we climb up a little bit higher
and see things from Heaven's perspective with the cross in view. We are
going to choose to take hold of one truth: we have the victory! We are the
triumphant ones in Christ. We are supernatural carriers of hope because of
Jesus. We have reason to overflow with gratitude all of our days, no matter
what this all looks like. We can face the giant or face the battle and write
the word "Triumph" over it. The story isn't done, and we know who wins!

*"The Lord will march out like a champion, like a warrior
he will stir up his zeal; with a shout he will raise the
battle cry and will triumph over his enemies."*
–Isaiah 42:13

Whatever your situation or trial is, see the word "Triumph" written over it. Receive that promise, even unfulfilled right now, fully complete in Christ!

I want us to look at the word "labor" in 1 Corinthians 15:58: *"… your labor in the Lord is not in vain."* The meaning behind this statement is that your labor in the Lord is not empty or resulting in nothing. Do you know that the word "labor" is actually associated with grief or sorrow and even trouble? It's interesting to me that Paul doesn't disregard this intimate part of being seated, persistent and firm, increasing and overflowing, and yet *"In this world you will have trouble,'"* Jesus said. *"But take heart! I have overcome the world (John 16:33).'"* **Yes, victory is ours, immovability is ours, increase is ours. And yet in this world, our labor or work can have pain, tears, and suffering associated with it.**

Being in the Lord and trusting you've heard clearly does not mean it won't come without tears and pain. In fact, you can count on two things: **every calling will be tested, and before every breakthrough, there will be a battle.** He sees the finished prize, and yet He rejoices in the process. He is faithful to carry us in the process. No one and nothing can snatch you from the hand of God. Come hell or high water, you are in Him, sealed with His Spirit, and He's coming back for you.

Your labor and your pain in the Lord are not in vain!

I need you to hear these words because, as we move from glory to glory, we become more like Jesus. He takes the areas of our lives that need to be shaped and pruned and purified, and if we will hand them to Him, we will put His glory on them. And we will look more and more like Jesus. Your pain and grief and sorrow are not in vain because you are in the Lord. Your God will never fail you; He will never forsake His own. Why? Because **your triumph was written by the blood of Jesus on the cross.**

"And what more shall I say? I do not have time to tell about Gideon, Barak, Samson and Jephthah, about David and Samuel and the prophets, who through faith conquered kingdoms, administered justice, and gained what was promised; who shut the mouths of lions, quenched the fury of the flames, and escaped the edge of the sword; whose weakness was turned to strength; and who became powerful in battle and routed foreign armies. Women received back their dead, raised to life again. There were others who were tortured, refusing to be released so that they might gain an even better resurrection. Some faced jeers and flogging, and even chains and imprisonment. They were put to death by stoning; they were sawed in two; they were killed by the sword. They went about in sheepskins and goatskins, destitute, persecuted and mistreated—the world was not worthy of them. They wandered in deserts and mountains, living in caves and in holes in the ground. These were all commended for their faith, yet none of them received what had been promised, since God had planned something better for us so that only together with us would they be made perfect."
—Hebrews 11:32–40

If you trust Him for the victory, will you trust Him in the trial?

Your labor in the Lord is not in vain. Even when we are walking in perfect union with Father, Jesus, and Holy Spirit, we are going to face toil and trial. We will begin to view it from the perspective of God the more we walk with Him in deeper intimacy. We will realize the necessity of gratitude to be the game changer for acceptance and embrace. And on the flip side of the pain will be the redemption of God. He will cause the pain and suffering to bring the overflow and even greater authority for ministry! The Lord is enlarging our capacity to carry more of His manifest power and presence through our lives. None of what you have gone through or are going through is in vain because you are in the Lord. But if it is not processed by the Word of God and the counsel of the Holy Spirit, this is where we can begin to believe the whispers of the enemy, and our faith can begin to waver.

So today, let's stand on the precipice of our tumultuous days and give Him praise. He knows how this story ends. Until we see that day come, our only option is to praise Him!

"Consider it pure joy, my brothers and sisters, whenever you face trials of many kinds, because you know that the testing of your faith produces perseverance. Let perseverance finish its work so that you may be mature and complete, not lacking anything."
–James 1:2–4

He is making you complete so that you will not be lacking anything. And the outcome of the pain is He will redeem and return to you sevenfold what the enemy has stolen. Take heart; you are secure in Him, and He is for you. Today, let's just praise Him and give Him thanks for His triumph and tenderness to His beloved Bride.

Thanks be to God for the victory in Christ Jesus!

COMMISSIONING PRAYER

Father, in the name of Jesus, I pray for every person who has read and worked and prayed and processed through these 40 days. Lord, I pray that you have done a work of reorienting their passions and pursuits to find their foundation in the person of Jesus. I pray that these ones will never fall away from the truth or from the Spirit. Keep their hearts anchored in You, Jesus. I pray that they would begin to dream with You and move with You, without hesitation. May these be ones who release the Kingdom of God in their generation and in this time in history for Your glory.

I pray for those who create. Lord, give them archetypes that come from the throne room of Heaven.

For those who run businesses, I pray that they would overflow with Kingdom resources so that entire nations are reached with the gospel.

I pray for our intercessors. Give them fervent perseverance in the secret place, and tune their ears to hear what You are interceding for, Jesus.

For our entrepreneurs, I pray for heavenly creativity, connections, and vision to plant Kingdom endeavors in the Earth.

I pray for our doctors and nurses to move in the power of the Holy Spirit so that the sick would be made well and miracles of healing would turn many hearts to Jesus.

I pray for those who faithfully go to the lost, and no one knows and no one sees but You, Lord. Protect them and anoint them to take new ground and proclaim the Kingdom of God with boldness.

Lord, I pray for a fresh anointing over women all over the globe. Raise them up as leaders in the Earth to birth gospel movements and raise up unwavering spiritual sons and daughters.

Would you pour out your Spirit on our men in this hour who will count their lives as nothing but knowing Christ and Him crucified. Raise them to be godly and consecrated unto You.

I pray for our worship leaders and worshippers throughout the Earth. May they sing the songs that are stirring Your heart in this hour to move powerfully on behalf of Your people.

Pour out fresh anointing on our apostles, prophets, evangelists, pastors, and teachers. Anchor them so that they are unwavering in this hour, for the sake of the Church.

Jesus, commission us afresh at the closing of these 40 days to burn for You. Set a fire that cannot be extinguished, and give us a love for the world You have died for. We need unwavering courage and deep resolve for the days ahead. When You return, find us knee-deep in Your harvest field, busy about Your work.

We love You and give You all the glory and all the praise! In Jesus' name! Amen!

About the Author

Julie King has been married to Michael for 29 years. They have had the privilege of watching their four daughters—Elizabeth, Emily, AnnMarie, and Grace—and their son-in-law, Patrick, grow and develop a passion for Jesus and have a heart for the nations. Her family is the delight of her life.

Julie grew up as a missionary kid to parents who served on staff with Cru for 33 years. Much of her youth was spent living overseas in Germany, during the fall of the Berlin Wall and the opening of the Iron Curtain. It was a formative period for both her worldview and passion for the gospel.

Today, Julie leads women around the world to take the gospel to people who have never heard the name of Jesus.

As an adult, Julie's desire and passion for the Bride of Christ and the lost—those who don't know Jesus personally—compelled her to begin a neighborhood Bible study to engage others in the Word and on mission. One result of this initiative was a prayer and worship gathering in Frisco, Texas, called God of the City: The Church unified-revived-unleashed. This three-year planting of the Lord was a movement to unite the church in North Dallas for the purpose of worship and prayer for revival. Hundreds of churches participated in the event, which was attended by thousands of people.

In 2018, Julie began an initiative called Arise through the mission of East-West. Through this effort, she is seeing women grow in a depth of hunger and passion for Jesus and His heart for the world. Julie serves as a full-time missionary with East-West.

Julie has a passion for the Word and for worship and loves rallying people to the very things God brings forth in her spirit. This book is a result of those passions, and she believes there's more to come.

ABOUT EAST-WEST

East-West began because two men couldn't resist the call of Christ's great mission: go into the world and make disciples (Matthew 28:18–20).

Through their work behind the Iron Curtain in the early 1980s, East-West founders John Maisel and Bud Toole recognized the profound need to train church planters and pastors in nations with severely restricted Christian activity.

In May 1993, East-West was established to train and mentor faithful and reliable national pastors to become catalysts for indigenous church growth—reaching the lost with the gospel, equipping new believers, and multiplying reproducible churches.

Today, East-West works primarily in limited-access countries and among unreached people groups in more than 54 countries worldwide so that disciples and churches will continuously multiply.

VISION
The vision of East-West is to glorify God by multiplying followers of Jesus in the spiritually darkest areas of the world.

MISSION

The mission of East-West is to mobilize the Body of Christ to evangelize the lost and equip local believers to multiply disciples and churches among the unreached.

GET INVOLVED

To learn more about East-West or to join the global ministry, visit www.eastwest.org.

ABOUT ARISE

Arise is an initiative born out of East-West's desire to empower women around the world to be used by God to take the gospel to the nations. This is done by calling, connecting, and commissioning them to one another and to the heart and purposes of God in this hour.

There is a call from the Lord for women right now to live in the authority and identity given to them by Christ. We are connecting women to each other through stories and experiences. And women are being commissioned to be a powerful force for the Kingdom of God.

That's why Arise exists.

We have a hopeful expectation that as we call women to live boldly in the power of the Holy Spirit, connect them to each other for ongoing encouragement, and send them out on their unique mission, a culture of revival will break loose as families, communities, and nations are changed forever for the glory of God.

Why? Because it's happened in the past.

Through women of our ancient past (such as Deborah, Ruth, Mary, and Lydia) and women of recent centuries (including Joan of Arc, Amy Carmichael, Corrie ten Boom, Mother Teresa, and Heidi Baker), God changed the world.

We believe that women who are moved by a passionate love for Jesus and who partner with Him to build His Kingdom are key to unlocking gospel movements in the world's spiritually dark places.

And now we are believing God for 70 cities nationally and internationally to build this Kingdom movement and mobilize women.

To learn more or to get involved with Arise, visit www.eastwest.org/arise.

Get Involved

It's time to discover your role in the Great Commission. Consider the following ways you can partner with East-West in God's Kingdom work.

PRAY: Prayer moves the mission. God works when we pray, which is why East-West is committed to passionate, consistent prayer for the unreached and our missionaries and national partners who serve among them. Prayer is our most powerful weapon against the kingdom of darkness; therefore, it is the greatest gift you can give to our ministry. You can join us in the important work of praying for those living in the throes of spiritual darkness as we seek to reach them with the good news of Jesus in a way that transforms their lives forever. Learn more about how you can partner with us in prayer at **www.eastwest.org/pray.**

GIVE: Your gift to East-West has eternal value. It continually expands our reach and multiples our impact as we seek to take the gospel to the lost. Each gift is an investment to reach the darkest areas of the world with the light of God's Word. With East-West, you are not investing in a fleeting kingdom of man but in an eternal Kingdom that cannot be shaken. You can give to the general ministry of East-West or East-West | Arise, to a missionary, to a region, or to a short-term mission team member. You can give now at **www.eastwest.org/give.**

 **GO:** Join the movement of the gospel throughout the nations by partnering with East-West on the field. Because the Great Commission is for every believer, we're committed to empowering the global Church to reach the unreached. Through short-term teams, missionary deployments, and mid-term opportunities, we train and send people just like you to take the gospel where it's never been. As believers go, we are witnessing God's Kingdom invade the spiritually darkest areas of the world. Explore the different ways you can go with East-West at **www.eastwest.org/go.**

NOTES

Day 4

[1] Schlink, M. Basilea. *My All for Him.* (Bethany House Pub, 2000)

Day 6

[2] Rankin, Jerry and Stetzer, Ed. *Spiritual Warfare and Missions: The Battle for God's Glory Among the Nations.* (Nashville: B&H Books, 2010)

Day 7

[3] Louis, Peter K. *Back to the Gospel: Reviving the Church through the Message that Birthed It.* (Braveheart Ministries, Inc., 2016)

Day 10

[4] Rankin, Jerry and Bridges, Erich. *Lives Given, Not Taken: 21st Century Southern Baptist Martyrs.* (2005)

Day 11

[5] Frangipane, Francis. *Holiness, Truth, and the Presence of God.* (Lake Mary: Charisma House, 2011)

Day 12

[6] Tsarfati, Amir. *Has the Tribulation Begun? Avoiding Confusion and Redeeming the Time in These Last days.* (Eugene: Harvest Prophecy, 2023)

Day 13

[7] Tsarfati, Amir. *Has the Tribulation Begun? Avoiding Confusion and Redeeming the Time in These Last days.* (Eugene: Harvest Prophecy, 2023)

Day 19

[8] Ahn, Ché. *Blueprints for Transformation, Bringing Revival and Reformation to the Nations.* (Pasadena: Servant Leader Publishing, 2024)

Day 23

[9] Murray, Andrew. *Absolute Surrender.* (1895)

Day 25

[10] Lewis, C.S. *The Screwtape Letters.* (United Kingdom: Geoffrey Bles, 1942)

Day 27

[11] Hibbs, Jack. *Living in the Daze of Deception.* (Eugene: Harvest House, 2024)

Day 32

[12] Hibbs, Jack. *Called to Take a Bold Stand, Resilient and Effective Faith for a Godless Age.* (Eugene: Harvest House, 2025)

Day 33, 34, 35, 36

[13] Ortland, Dane. *Deeper: Real Change for Real Sinners.* (Wheaton: Crossway, 2021)

Day 39

[14] Rankin, Jerry. *A Challenge to Great Commission Obedience: Motivational Messages for Contemporary Missionaries.* (B&H Books, 2006)

WORKS CITED

Ahn, Ché. *Blueprints for Transformation, Bringing Revival and Reformation to the Nations.* (Pasadena: Servant Leader Publishing, 2024)

Frangipane, Francis. *Holiness, Truth, and the Presence of God.* (Lake Mary: Charisma House, 2011)

Hibbs, Jack. *Called to Take a Bold Stand, Resilient and Effective Faith for a Godless Age.* (Eugene: Harvest House, 2025)

Hibbs, Jack. *Living in the Daze of Deception.* (Eugene: Harvest House, 2024)

Lewis, C.S. *The Screwtape Letters.* (United Kingdom: Geoffrey Bles, 1942)

Louis, Peter K. *Back to the Gospel: Reviving the Church through the Message that Birthed It.* (Braveheart Ministries, Inc., 2016)

Murray, Andrew. *Absolute Surrender.* (1895)

Ortland, Dane. *Deeper: Real Change for Real Sinners.* (Wheaton: Crossway, 2021)

Rankin, Jerry. *A Challenge to Great Commission Obedience: Motivational Messages for Contemporary Missionaries.* (B&H Books, 2006)

Rankin, Jerry and Bridges, Erich. *Lives Given, Not Taken: 21st Century Southern Baptist Martyrs.* (2005)

Rankin, Jerry and Stetzer, Ed. *Spiritual Warfare and Missions: The Battle for God's Glory Among the Nations.* (Nashville: B&H Books, 2010)

Schlink, M. Basilea. *My All for Him.* (Bethany House Pub, 2000)

Tsarfati, Amir. *Has the Tribulation Begun? Avoiding Confusion and Redeeming the Time in These Last days.* (Eugene: Harvest Prophecy, 2023)